1 CORINTHIANS:
DISPENSATIONALLY CONSIDERED

A GRACE EXPOSITIONAL COMMENTARY

SECOND EDITION

DR. DAVID ALAN GREENE

GraceWord Publishing, LLC
www.gracewordpublishing.com
U.S.A.

GRACEWORD PUBLISHING

Contents

To My Grandchildren Sarah and Gabriel

And now abideth
faith, hope, charity, these three;
but the greatest of these
is charity.

- Apostle Paul

Acknowledgements

I would like to take a moment to thank both my parents Harold Alan and Frances Greene who encouraged me to continue my education and attain my degrees. Jon and Susan McMahon, my brother and sister in Christ, continue to encourage me in my writing.

I would also like to express my gratitude to Rev. Steven Tackett who is always willing to discuss the biblical text. Finally, a special thanks to Barbara Pennington, Frances Greene, and Janice Jewell who assisted me in the editing process.

Introduction

There is an approach to understanding Scripture that puts the entire Bible into a simple system of interpretation. The argument is that to understand God's Word we must reason from the general to the specific and not from the specific to the general. To choose only parts of Paul's epistles and read them apart from their biblical context gets people into trouble with their interpretation. It would be looking at specific verses detached from the general structure or framework of Scripture.

God created a timeline or eternal plan for the restoration of His Creation. This plan is first mentioned in Genesis. It is the *protoevangelium* or the first announcement of good news. God speaks to the Serpent who is Satan in verse 3:15:

> **15 And I will put enmity between thee [the Serpent] and the woman, and between thy seed and <u>her seed</u>; it shall bruise thy head, and thou shalt**

bruise his heel.

The word *seed* can be either singular or plural. Here, "it" is singular and refers specifically to *the Seed,* Who is Christ. Also, notice that it is the woman's seed because it was given to her by God directly. This is often called the *immaculate conception* or the divine impregnation of the virgin Mary with the holy *Seed.* This is the very first promise of good news and will remain the central theme throughout the entire Bible. It is said to be like a scarlet thread woven throughout Scripture. It is this *Seed* Who will ultimately redeem Creation!

God does things methodically as He patiently works His plan of restoration. He makes Himself known to man through a series of progressive revelations. Timothy was a student preacher trained by Paul. His letters to both Timothy and Titus are referred to as the *pastoral epistles* because he is instructing these young pastors. Paul wants Timothy to understand Scripture and teach it correctly. Doing so, he will not be ashamed or embarrassed. 2 Timothy 2:15:

> 15 <u>Study to shew thyself approved</u> unto God, a workman that needeth not to be ashamed, <u>rightly dividing the word of truth.</u>

The Greek word translated as *rightly dividing* is *orthotomeo*. It is a compound word comprised of *ortho* which mean *correct* or *with great precision* and the word *tomeo* which is the verb *to cut*. Another example would be *orthodox*. Again, *ortho* means *correct* or *with great precision*. *Dox* means *doctrine* or *teaching*. When combined *orthodox* means *correct doctrine*. The last example is a medical procedure which includes the cutting out or removal of something. In its name, the suffix *-ectomy* is added. The Greek *ek* which means *out* attached to the verb *tomeo* means *to cut out*. This is a lot of detail to make a point that Paul is clearly saying to Timothy that he needs to carefully and correctly *cut* or *divide* the *Word of Truth*.

Therefore, this concept of *carefully dividing Scripture*, when applied correctly, makes a huge difference on its interpretation! The Bible is the sum of its parts. These parts or divisions of the Bible are referred to as *dispensations*. In Greek, the word is *oikonomia*. It is also a compound word. It is comprised of *oikos* meaning *household* and *nomos* meaning *law or rule*. *Oikonomia* is a compound word which is the origin of our word *economy*. A president rules or administrates the country and its economy by certain laws. Therefore, a *dispensation* is a period of time in which God *dispenses* or administrates His household.

This brief summary of *dispensation* does not do it justice. For a deeper explanation, I would recommend you read *Letters To Theophilus* which handles the subject in greater detail. It explains all seven dispensations in God's plan for restoration. There are two dispensation which are critical to our understanding the book of Corinthians. Presently, we are in what some call the *Church Age*. However, I would not like to use this name because the word *church* has too many uses. I prefer the name *Age of Grace* because this is the very core of its message.

Paul is the only one who uses the word *dispensation* in the Bible. It is used in the following verses:

1 Corinthians 9:17:

> 17 **For if I do this thing willingly, I have a reward: but if against my will, <u>a dispensation of the gospel is committed unto me</u>.**

Ephesians 1:10:

> 10 **That in <u>the dispensation of the fulness of times</u> he might gather together in one all things in Christ, both which are in heaven, and which are on earth; even [that is to say] in him:**

Ephesians 3:2:

> 2 **If ye have heard of <u>the dispensation of the grace of God</u> which is given me to you-ward [for you]:**

Colossians 1:25:

> 25 **Whereof I am made a minister, according to <u>the dispensation of God</u> which is given to me for you, to fulfil the word of God;**

These verses should not be interpreted out of context. They are solely presented here as evidence of Paul's use of the word *dispensation* in his epistles.

Many theologians have *divided* the Bible into seven dispensations. Notice that this is the same as the number of days of Creation. For our purpose, we will concentrate on only two dispensations: the *Age of Law* and the *Age of Grace*. Under the Mosaic Covenant, Israel obligated itself to keeping the Law. The weight of the Law proved to be too much for them. The Gentiles, or non-Jews, were outside of this covenantal agreement. Following the Jews' rejection of their Messiah, in the last chapter of Acts, Paul makes a proclamation. Acts 28:28-29:

28 **Be it known therefore unto you, that** <u>**the salvation of God is sent unto the**</u> <u>**Gentiles,**</u> **and that** <u>**they will hear it.**</u> 29 **And when he had said these words, the Jews departed, and had great reasoning among themselves.**

The Apostle Paul wrote thirteen epistles or letters in the New Testament. Each letter was written to a group of believers or to specific individuals such as Philemon, Titus, and Timothy. All of these letters, with the exception of Romans, were written to people Paul had met personally. Many of them he lived with while teaching them face to face. Therefore, most recipients of these letters had a general understanding of his doctrine before receiving his letter.

The letter to the Romans was different. Some believers had heard Paul and believed. Then, they relocated to the capitol city of Rome. Many who had not met or heard Paul teach had become believers through the testimony of others. Romans was written to provide a foundational basis of Paul's doctrine. Upon the substance of Romans are all his other letters written. For that reason, it is placed first in the series of his epistles.

I like to use this as an example. Take a moment and think about a multi-part series of some epic story. How difficult would it be to understand the full depth of a story by starting in the middle of season three? It would be difficult to understand it. For this same reason, we will consider the unique gospel message which Paul preached. We must not confuse or combine his distinct message with the message preached by the Twelve! Paul made three missionary trips to proclaim this gospel. His final trip would end in Rome where he would be executed. Many of his later letters were written while he was a prisoner in Rome awaiting his trial.

The Apostle Paul preached a unique gospel message. Scripture confirms he personally received this from the Risen Savior. The information he received was a mystery and, therefore, had never been disclosed to anyone until it was disclosed to him. In fact, this message Paul received was specifically directed to the Gentiles. Let us consider the evidence. Scripture records his confrontation with the Risen Savior on the Road to Damascus in Acts 9:3-9:

> 3 **And as he journeyed, he came near Damascus: and suddenly there shined round about him a light from heaven:**
> 4 **And he fell to the earth, and heard a voice saying unto him, Saul, Saul, why persecutest thou me?**

5 And he said, <u>Who art thou, Lord?</u> And the Lord said, <u>I am Jesus whom thou persecutest</u>: it is hard for thee to kick against the pricks.

6 And he trembling and astonished said, Lord, what wilt thou have me to do? And the Lord said unto him, Arise, and go into the city, and it shall be told thee what thou must do. 7 And the men which journeyed with him stood speechless, hearing a voice, but seeing no man.

8 And Saul arose from the earth; and when his eyes were opened, he saw no man: but they led him by the hand, and brought him into Damascus. 9 And he was three days without sight, and neither did eat nor drink.

The Apostle Paul had never met Jesus during His earthly ministry. Therefore, he could not fulfill the requirements for the replacement of Judas as the twelfth apostle. (*cf.* Acts 1:21-26.)

In Damascus, God directs a faithful disciple named Ananias to heal Paul's blindness. Pay close attention to this dialogue between God and Ananias.

Acts 9:10-16

10 And there was a certain disciple at Damascus, named Ananias; and to him said the Lord in a vision, Ananias. And he said, Behold, I am here, Lord. 11 And the Lord said unto him, Arise, and go into the street which is called Straight, and enquire in the house of Judas for one called Saul, of Tarsus: for, behold, he prayeth, 12 And hath seen in a vision a man named Ananias coming in, and putting his hand on him, that he might receive his sight.

13 Then Ananias answered, Lord, I have heard by many of this man, <u>how much evil he hath done to thy saints at Jerusalem</u>: 14 And here he hath author-ity from the chief priests to bind all that call on thy name. 15 But the Lord said unto him, <u>Go thy way: for he is a chosen vessel unto me, to bear my name before the Gentiles, and kings, and the children of Israel:</u>

16 <u>For I will shew him how great things he must suffer for my name's sake.</u>

In Paul's letter to the Galatians, he writes something he had most likely shared with other believers in person. These verses below recall his second meeting with the other apostles in Jerusalem. Paul had only met Peter and James on his previous trip and none of the others. Galatians 2:1-9:

1 **Then fourteen years after I went up again to Jerusalem with Barnabas, and took Titus with me also.** 2 **And I went up by revelation, and communicated unto them that gospel which I preach among the Gentiles, but privately to them which were of reputation, lest [for fear that] by any means I should run, or had run, in vain.**

3 **But neither Titus, who was with me, being a Greek, was compelled to be circumcised:** 4 **And that because of false brethren unawares brought in, who came in privily to spy out our liberty which we have in Christ Jesus, that they might bring us into bondage:** 5 **To whom we gave place by subjection, no, not for an hour; that the truth of the gospel might continue with you.**

6 **But of these who seemed to be some-**

what [of importance], (whatsoever they were, it maketh no matter to me: God accepteth no man's person:) for they who seemed to be somewhat in conference added nothing to me:

7 But contrariwise, when they saw that the gospel of the uncircumcision was committed unto me, as the gospel of the circumcision was unto Peter; 8 (For he that wrought effectually in Peter to the apostleship of the circumcision, the same was mighty in me toward the Gentiles:)

9 And when James, Cephas, and John, who seemed to be pillars, perceived the grace that was given unto me, they gave to me and Barnabas the right hands of fellowship; that we should go unto the heathen [Gentiles], and they unto the circumcision [Jews].

Paul provides a concise statement of this gospel he was to deliver to the Gentiles. We find it in 1 Corinthians. Notice his use of the definite article *the* when referring to *the* gospel. This is the *Gospel of Grace* in its simplest form. It is the basis of the Gentile's salvation. 1 Corinthians 15:1-4:

1 Moreover, brethren, I declare unto you <u>the</u> gospel which I preached unto you, which also ye have received, and <u>wherein ye stand;</u> 2 <u>By which also ye are saved</u>, if ye keep in memory what I preached unto you, unless ye have believed in vain.

3 <u>For I delivered unto you first of all that which I also received,</u> [1] how that Christ died for our sins according to the scriptures; 4 [2] And that he was buried, and [3] that he rose again the third day according to the scriptures:

We must always remember the simplicity of the *Gospel of Grace*. It consists of Christ's death on the Cross, His burial, and His resurrection. It is *by faith* or *the believing of these facts* that anyone can receive salvation! His death, burial, and resurrection allows God to *justify sinners!* Those who believe by faith, God justifies—are *proclaimed not guilty!* All this is possible because of what God had accomplished through the completed work of Christ!

The sufficiency of Christ's completed work on the Cross is critical to the *Gospel of Grace*. This cannot be over emphasized. Nothing must be added. Paul makes this clear in all his letters. This is one of the most quoted verses from Paul's writings. Ephesians 2:8-9:

> 8 **For by grace are ye saved through faith; and that not of yourselves: <u>it is the gift of God</u>:** 9 <u>**Not of works**</u>**, lest [for fear that] any man should boast.**

In his letter to the Galatians, he chastised some of them because they had added works as a requirement for salvation. Today, many Christians will add the requirement of works to the simplicity of salvation by grace through faith! Paul warns the believers in Colossae. Colossians 2:8:

> 8 **Beware lest any man spoil you through <u>philosophy</u> and <u>vain deceit</u>, after the <u>tradition of men</u>, after the <u>rudiments of the world</u>, and not after Christ.**

Paul's gospel message is separate and distinct from the Twelve. In Galatians, he affirms that he did not receive it from any of the other apostles or, for that matter, from any other man. He affirms he received it directly from the Risen Savior. Galatians 1:11-12:

> 11 **But I certify you, brethren, that the gospel which was preached of [by] me**

is not after [from] man. 12 For I neither received it of man, neither was I taught it, but by the revelation of Jesus Christ.

When growing up I remember asking my Methodist pastor why he did not preach from Paul's letters. He told me that it was because Paul had persecuted the Church and, therefore, he was taught to avoid him. Another pastor told me that Paul's writings were only his opinion and, therefore, not reliable. Friend, either Scripture is inspired, infallible, and complete or it is not. The Bible is our only source of truth. It is trustworthy and we have God's Word on it.

Paul was indeed an enemy of God. He admits this because he persecuted the Kingdom Believers. Galatians 1:13-14:

13 For ye have heard of my conversation [manner of living] <u>in time past in the Jews' religion, how that beyond meas-ure I persecuted the church of God, and wasted it</u>: 14 And profited in the Jews' religion above many my equals in mine own nation, being more exceedingly zealous of the traditions of my fathers.

This is great news for people who, like myself, are sinners. For if God can save Paul, then He can save anyone who is willing to believe. He continues with verses 15-17:

> 15 **But <u>when it pleased God</u>, who separated me from my mother's womb, and called me by his grace, 16 <u>To reveal his Son in [to] me, that I might preach him among the heathen</u> [Gentiles]; immediately <u>I conferred not with flesh and blood</u> [any man]: 17 <u>Neither went I up to Jerusalem to them which were apostles before me</u>; but [instead] I went into Arabia, and [later] returned again unto Damascus.**

God set Paul apart for a special ministry to the Gentiles. This did not mean that the offer of the *Gospel of Grace* was not also open to the Jews. It is available to everyone but only effective for those who believe. Paul continually refers to *faith* or *the act of believing* as the requirement for salvation throughout his epistles.

Here is something for those who are new to the concept that Paul's gospel is different from the other Twelve. Find a large jumbo paper clip. Now, beginning with the last page of Acts and ending with the first page of Hebrews place the large paper clip over those pages in between. The pages contained within the paper clip should begin with Romans and end with Philemon. These thirteen epistles were written by Paul. In a moment, you will see how this makes sense.

Take a look at the last chapter of Acts which immediately precedes Paul's first book. While Paul is incarcerated in Rome, he calls the local Jewish leaders to meet with him. (*cf.* Acts 28:16-30.) After reasoning with them at great length, they leave undecided and are arguing amongst themselves. At this point, notice that Paul makes a declaration. Acts 28:28:

28 **Be it known therefore unto you, that** **the salvation of God is sent unto the** **Gentiles, and** **that they will hear it.**

Is it interesting that these are the words which end the portion of Scripture immediately preceding Paul's epistles? Now, let us look at the other side of the paperclip. Turn to the portion of Scripture which follows Paul's epistles. You will come to the book of Hebrews. Seeing a pattern here yet? Hebrews is written to *believing Israel!* They are the Jewish believers who follow the teaching of the Twelve. They are following the *Gospel of the Kingdom* preached by Christ and the Twelve!

The gospel which Paul received from the Lord Jesus Christ is directed to the Gentiles! It is called *the Gospel of Grace* for a reason. *Grace* means *gift*. Therefore, it is God's gift to anyone who, by *faith,* believes what God has already done for you. Because of His Son's death, burial, and resurrection, God is graciously offering salvation as a gift to anyone who believes. Why? Christ paid the price in full!

Therefore, it is critical for our purpose, as we seek to understand Paul's writings, that we understand the two dispensations. They are the *Age of Law* and the *Age of Grace*. Most pastors and teachers of the Bible believe that these two dispensation are sequential. In other words, they believe that one dispensation follows the other, but this is not true. The *Age of Law* began with Moses and the nation of Israel. They contractually accepted and were bound by the Mosaic Covenant. This covenant was still in effect at the time of Jesus' ministry. Matthew 5:17

> 17 **Think not that I am come to destroy the law, or the prophets: <u>I am not come to destroy, but to fulfil [the Law].</u>**

However, Paul's message is different. It is about grace and, therefore, must not be mingled with the Law! He writes this to grace believers in Galatians 2:21:

21 I do not frustrate the grace of God: <u>for if righteousness come by the law, then Christ is dead in vain.</u>

The *Age of Law* is temporarily suspended and will resume at the close of the *Age of Grace*. This is referred to as a *parenthetical interruption*. The prophetic program given in Daniel 9 is currently held in abeyance until this present age, the *Age of Grace*, is completed. We are introduced to Paul, named Saul at that time, at the stoning of Stephen. Shortly after that, the *Age of Grace* began with the conversion of Paul. He was *the first to be saved by grace through faith.* The *Age of Grace* will end at *His Calling* of those saved by His grace through faith—the *Rapture*.

With this brief summary of the *Age of Grace* and Paul's unique gospel message, we are ready to begin our study of 1 Corinthians.

1

Corinth

We first hear about Corinth and its association to the Apostle Paul when we read Acts 18. If you envision the bottom of Greece extending south into the Mediterranean Sea, then you would see Athens located on the bottom right. There they have warm breezes as well as tempests off the sea. On a small isthmus connecting what would have been a large island, the city of Corinth is located a little over forty miles west of Athens. Similar to other areas in this region, we find from Luke's writings there was a sizeable Jewish populus in this region. We will turn to the biblical record to give us additional details.

When writing to the grace believers in Rome, he said, "But glory, honour, and peace, to every man that worketh good, to the Jew first, and also to the Gentile" (Rom. 2:10). This was Paul's custom. Therefore, when he arrives in Corinth, he goes to the Jews first. Acts 18:1-4.

> 1 **After these things Paul departed from Athens, and came to Corinth; 2 And found a certain Jew named Aquila, born in Pontus, lately come from Italy, with his wife Priscilla; (because that [Emperor] Claudius had commanded all Jews to depart from Rome:) and came unto them.**

> 3 **And because he was of the same craft [trade], he abode with them, and wrought [worked]: for by their occupation they were tentmakers. 4 And he reasoned [with the Jews] in the synagogue every sabbath, and persuaded the Jews and the Greeks.**

Each time Paul presents the Jews with the gospel, it is rarely received well. Once Silas and Timothy arrived, the Spirit urged him to do this also in Corinth. Verses 5-9:

> 5 **And when Silas and Timotheus were come from Macedonia, Paul was pressed [urged] in the spirit, and testified to the Jews that Jesus was [the]**

Christ. 6 **And when they opposed themselves, and blasphemed, he shook his raiment, and said unto them, Your blood be upon your own heads; I am clean: from henceforth I will go unto the Gentiles.**

However, Paul remains in Corinth at the house of Justus which was, coincidentally, adjacent to the local synagogue. Verses 7-11:

7 **And he departed thence, and entered into a certain man's house, named Justus, one that worshipped God, whose house joined hard to the synagogue.** 8 **And Crispus, the chief ruler of the synagogue, believed on the Lord with all his house; and many of the Corinthians hearing believed, and were baptized.**

Although there is going to be opposition, God assures Paul that he will be protected among the believers there and he should not fear. Verses 9-11:

9 **Then spake the Lord to Paul in the night by a vision, Be not afraid, but speak, and hold not thy peace:** 10 **For I am with thee, and no man shall set on**

thee to hurt thee: for I have much [many] people in this city. 11 And he continued there a year and six months, teaching the word of God among them.

There is nothing like the assurance of God in the time of adversity. Paul remained there in Corinth for eighteen months ministering to them and writing his letters.

Rome governs by region and makes appointments of various governors or overseers who are to administrate their regions. Any issues or problems arising there are to be brought to this administrator. Such is the case below in which the Jews brought charges against Paul for subversion. Remembering God's promise to Paul, look at how it is handled. Not only are the charges never adjudicated, but look at how those making the accusation were dealt with by the Greeks! Verses 12-17:

12 And when Gallio was the deputy of Achaia, the Jews made insurrection with one accord against Paul, and brought him to the judgment seat, 13 Saying, This fellow persuadeth men to worship God contrary to the law.

14 And when Paul was now about to

open his mouth, Gallio said unto the Jews, If it were a matter of wrong or wicked lewdness, O ye Jews, reason would that I should bear with you: 15 But if it be a question of words and names, and of your law, look ye to it; for I will be no judge of such matters.

16 And he drave [drove] them from the judgment seat [court]. 17 Then all the Greeks took Sosthenes, the chief ruler of the synagogue, and beat him before the judgment seat. And Gallio cared for none of those things.

God made an example of Sosthenes and, thereafter, few would bring trouble upon Paul.

Feeling more confident and protected, Paul was able to remain there until he was called to his next destination. Verses 18-21:

18 And Paul after this tarried there yet a good while, and then took his leave of the brethren, and sailed thence into Syria, and [took] with him Priscilla and Aquila; having shorn his head in Cenchrea: for he had a vow. 19 And he came to Ephesus, and left them there:

**but he himself entered into the syna-
gogue, and reasoned with the Jews.**

**20 When they desired him to tarry longer
time with them, he consented not; 21 But
bade them farewell, saying, I must by
all means keep this feast that cometh in
Jerusalem: but I will return again unto
you, if God will. And he sailed from
Ephesus.**

When Paul left Corinth, he brought with him
Priscilla and Aquila and left them in Ephesus. He
was bound for Jerusalem having determined to fulfill a promise he had made. His shaved head was to
remind him of this pledge made at his meeting with
the other apostles. (*cf.* Gal 2:8-10.) He promised he
would *remember the poor* and had taken up a collection among the grace assemblies. It was his promise
to deliver this collection himself.

The Jews who, since Acts 2, had remained in
Jerusalem believed Christ to be their Messiah. They
had followed *the Gospel of the Kingdom*. They were
poor because they sold all their belongings to distrib-
ute among those in need as directed by the Twelve.
At the time, the arrival of the promised Kingdom
was *at hand* or imminent and remained so until the
stoning of Stephen. To understand the significance of

this event, you should read chapters 6 and 7 of Acts which recounts the entire story. Stephen's impassioned speech before the Sanhedrin was an indictment of the leadership of Israel. Here we have their response. Acts 7:57-58:

> 57 Then they cried out with a loud voice, and stopped their ears, and ran upon him [Stephen] with one accord, 58 <u>And cast him out of the city, and stoned him: and the witnesses laid down their clothes at a young man's feet, whose name was Saul.</u>

Do you remember the one sin Jesus Christ told the Jews would not be forgiven? It is blasphemy of the Holy Spirit. Matthew 12:31-32:

> 31 Wherefore I say unto you, All manner of sin and blasphemy shall be forgiven unto men: <u>but the blasphemy against the Holy Ghost shall not be forgiven unto men.</u> 32 And whosoever speaketh a word against the Son of man, it shall be forgiven him: <u>but whosoever speaketh against the Holy Ghost, it shall not be forgiven him, neither in this world, neither in the world to come.</u>

Let us look at what, I believe, caused the temporary suspension of the Kingdom Prophecy. See an important fact stated here. Acts 6:15:

> **15 And <u>all that sat in the council</u>, looking stedfastly on him, saw his face as it had been the face of an angel.**

It is important that you see the words *all that sat in the council*. In other words, *all the leadership of Israel saw this*. Stephen was filled with the Holy Spirit.

We will read Stephen's summation against them. Acts 7:51-53:

> **51 Ye [All you] stiffnecked and un-circumcised in heart and ears, ye do always resist the Holy Ghost: as your fathers did, so do ye. 52 Which of the prophets have not your fathers persecuted? and they have slain them which shewed before of the coming of the Just One; of whom ye have been now the betrayers and murderers: 53 Who have received the law by the disposition of angels, and have not kept it.**

They were convicted! They were *cut to the heart!*

Now, let us consider their reaction. Were they repentant? Sorrowful? Under *the Age of Grace* all sins are forgiven, but not so under *the Age of Law*. Look at their reaction! Verses 54-58:

> 54 **When they heard these things, <u>they were cut to the heart</u>, and they gnashed on him with their teeth. 55 But he [Stephen], being full of the Holy Ghost, looked up stedfastly into heaven, and saw the glory of God, and Jesus standing on the right hand of God,**

> 56 **And said, Behold, I see the heavens opened, and the Son of man standing on the right hand of God. 57 Then <u>they cried out with a loud voice, and stopped their ears, and ran upon him</u> with one accord, 58 And cast him out of the city, and stoned him: and the witnesses laid down their clothes at a young man's feet, <u>whose name was Saul.</u>**

If this were a play, the curtain would fall with Paul who was giving consent to Stephen's death. He would be standing there with the cloaks of Stephen's murderers at his feet.

In a scene that follows, the curtain rises upon

the confrontation between the Risen Lord and Saul. Saul is blinded and will not receive his sight for three days. The man who was once an enemy of Christ persecuting His followers has now been chosen to be the pattern. Paul is the example for all who will be saved by grace through faith to follow. Think about this. If God can save Paul who was the *chief of sinners*, the worst of the worst, then He can save anyone without exception!

Paul believed God and, like Abraham, God counted his faith to him as righteousness. Friend, this applies to everyone who places their faith in the finished work of Christ's death, burial, and resurrection. This is the gospel message first given to Paul, the Apostle to the Gentiles. It is this message which God entrusted to him.

2

1 Corinthians 1

Do you remember Sosthenes mentioned in the previous chapter? Look at the beginning of this letter. Paul includes Sosthenes in his greetings. He is now a beloved brother in Christ! 1 Corinthians 1:1:

> 1 **Paul, called to be an apostle of Jesus Christ through the will of God, and Sosthenes our brother,**

Like a memo is written today, it includes the *From* and *To* at the beginning. He writes to the believers in the assembly in Corinth. Believers are to be sanctified or separated from the world. Here, those who are *sanctified* are called *saints*. Verse 2:

> 2 **Unto the church of God which is at Corinth, to them that are sanctified in**

Christ Jesus, called to be saints, with all that in every place call upon the name of Jesus Christ our Lord, both theirs and ours:

As is his custom, he includes in his salutation words which are unique to his gospel message. Verse 3:

3 **<u>Grace</u> be unto you, <u>and peace,</u> from God our Father, and from the Lord Jesus Christ.**

Having received the gift of salvation by grace, those who were once enemies with God now have peace with Him. Consider the following verses:

Romans 5:1:

1 **Therefore <u>being justified by faith,</u> <u>we have peace with God</u> through our Lord Jesus Christ:**

Romans 5:9-10:

9 **Much more then, <u>being now justified by his blood,</u> <u>we shall be saved from wrath through him.</u> 10 For if, when we were enemies, <u>we were reconciled to God by the death of his Son,</u> much**

**more, being reconciled, we shall be
saved by his life.**

Paul is grateful to God for each person who believes his message. He thinks of them as his children
in the faith. His ministry is difficult. It is hard to im-
agine how challenging it is to give away salvation for
free. Everyone wants to earn it by doing works and,
yet, it is a gift! 1 Corinthians 1:4:

> **4 I thank my God always on your behalf,
> for the grace of God which is given [to]
> you by Jesus Christ;**

Grace means gift. There should never be a charge or
cost for something received as a gift, right? This gift
of salvation is received by believing what God has
already done for us through His Son. Paul continues
by telling them their lives are seen as a witness of
Christ's effect upon them. It is evident from their
speech and actions. Verses 5-6:

> **5 That in every thing ye are enriched by
> him [Christ], in all utterance, and in all
> knowledge; 6 Even [That is to say] as the
> testimony of Christ was confirmed in
> you:**

Their lives are different from those who are not

saved. People notice this. It is their personal testimony.

Confident they received salvation, Paul wants to make sure they do not miss out on the blessings. One of those blessing is the Rapture which he mentions in the following verses. Here, he uses the phrases *the coming of our Lord Jesus Christ* and *the day of our Lord Jesus Christ* to refer to the same thing. It can also be described as *His Calling*. Verses 7-8:

> 7 **So that ye come behind in no gift; waiting for <u>the coming of our Lord Jesus Christ</u>:** 8 **Who shall also <u>confirm you unto the end</u>, that ye may be blameless in <u>the day of our Lord Jesus Christ</u>.**

It is God Who gave His Son. His Son did the work and, as believers, by faith we receive His gift of salvation. There are other gifts beyond salvation. Paul wants to make sure the Corinthians do not miss out on them. Since these are also gifts, then they must be free also. For gifts are free and require no payment or obligation. Verse 9:

> 9 **God is faithful, by whom ye were called unto the fellowship of his Son Jesus Christ our Lord.**

Paul wants unity in the doctrine and message they share. He wants them to be in agreement by being of one mind and one judgment. Verse 10:

> 10 **Now I beseech you, brethren, by the name of our Lord Jesus Christ, that ye all speak the same thing, and that there be no divisions among you; but that ye be perfectly joined together in the same mind and in the same judgment.**

He is writing this because he heard there are disagreements among them. Verses 11-13:

> 11 **For it hath been declared unto me of [concerning] you, my brethren, by [from] them which are of the house of Chloe, that there are contentions among you. 12 Now this I say, that every one of you saith, I am of Paul; and I of Apollos; and I of Cephas; and I of Christ. 13 Is Christ divided? was Paul crucified for you? or were ye baptized in the name of Paul?**

Each of them says they follow someone different whether Paul, Apollos, or Cephas who is Peter, while others say they follow Christ. He asks this question, "Is Christ divided?" In spite of who it was that taught them, he urges them to be united and follow Christ.

Peter and the others continued to follow Christ's instructions known as the Great Commission. Matthew 28:19-20:

> 19 **Go ye therefore, and teach all nations, baptizing them in the name of the Father, and of the Son, and of the Holy Ghost: 20 <u>Teaching them to observe all things whatsoever I have commanded you</u>: and, lo, I am with you alway, even unto the end of the world. Amen.**

Keeping or doing the commandments is a requirement for salvation under the Kingdom Gospel. However, Paul's gospel includes no such requirements. At the beginning of his ministry he preached to the Jews. Due to the great difficulty and rejection, Paul would turn to the Gentiles in his latter ministry. Paul rejoices that he initially baptized only a few of them. 1 Corinthians 1:14-17:

> 14 **I thank God that I baptized none of you, but Crispus and Gaius; 15 Lest any should say that I had baptized in mine own name. 16 And I baptized also the household of Stephanas: besides, I**

know not whether I baptized any other. 17 For Christ sent me not to baptize, but to preach the gospel: not with wisdom of words, lest the cross of Christ should be made of none effect.

Paul was given a very specific mission. He asks the Ephesians for prayer concerning this mission. Ephesians 6:19:

> **19 And for me, that utterance may be given unto me, that I may open my mouth boldly, to make known the mystery of the gospel,**

I mentioned the difficulty of trying to offer salvation for free. It is free because Someone else paid for our salvation for us! Paul explains what makes this so difficult. 1 Corinthians 1:18-19:

> **18 For the preaching of the cross is to them that perish foolishness; but unto us which are saved it is the power of God. 19 For it is written, I will destroy the wisdom of the wise, and will bring to nothing the understanding of the prudent.**

He compares this to the *wisdom of the wise* and the

understanding of the prudent. Both of these phrases refer to what some call *science* which is the knowledge of and understanding of the learned. In his first letter to the Corinthians, Paul uses the word *foolishness* six times. *Foolishness* means *a lack of understanding, wisdom, or good judgment.*

He continues by explaining why the simplicity of the Gospel of Grace is such a problem for the world. Verses 20-21:

> 20 **Where is the wise? where is the scribe? where is the disputer of this world? hath [has] not God made foolish the wisdom of this world? 21 For after that in the wisdom of God the world by wisdom knew not God, it pleased God by the foolishness of preaching [by preaching grace] <u>to save them that believe.</u>**

That is the stumbling block for most people. It does not make sense from the worldly perspective. To the wise and learned the wisdom of the world sees the simplicity of the Gospel of Grace as foolishness!

Paul addresses two groups. The Jews worship the true Creator of the universe. Then, there were the Gentiles or non-Jews. He refers to them as Greeks because their god is rational thought, vain philosophy of men, and the pursuit of worldly knowledge. Verses 22-23:

> 22 For <u>the Jews require a sign,</u> and <u>the Greeks seek after wisdom:</u> 23 But we preach Christ crucified, <u>unto the Jews a stumblingblock,</u> and <u>unto the Greeks foolishness;</u>

He now compares this with those who heard and believed God's offer of salvation by grace. Verse 24:

> 24 But <u>unto them which are called,</u> both Jews and Greeks, <u>Christ [is] the power of God, and the wisdom of God.</u>

When you see the words *the power of God* it refers to the same power God used to create something out of nothing! It is also the power He used to bring to life He Who was dead! Verse 25:

> 25 Because the foolishness of God is wiser than men; and the weakness of God is stronger than men.

For the Corinthians did receive something that few others are willing to receive. When Paul uses the word *called*, he is speaking about those who listened to the gospel, heard His offer, and accepted His *calling*. It was a choice they made according to their own free will. He mentions the wise, the mighty, and the noble in verse 26:

> 26 **For ye see [heard and understood] your calling**, brethren, how that not many wise men after the flesh [worldly], not many mighty, not many noble, are called:

The simplicity of God's offer of salvation is not what the world expects. It is not based upon their worldly views or understanding. Verse 27:

> 27 But God hath chosen **the foolish things of the world to confound the wise**; and God hath chosen **the weak things of the world to confound the things which are mighty;**

He speaks about the wise and the powerful above. In the following, the phrase *base things* refers to that which is *low in value or estimation* according to the measures of the world. Verse 28:

> 28 And base things of the world, and things which are despised, hath God

chosen, yea, and things which are not, to bring to nought [nothing the] things that are:

Let us stop for a moment and think about how God chose to solve the problem of sin and its related judgment. The pride of life was created by Adam when he, like Satan, chose to be *like God*. Since then, fallen men have desired to be like God. Only those who are humble enough to admit they are incapable of obtaining the solution and know that only God can provide the solution will be saved. Paul explains the reason for the simplicity of God's solution. Verses 29-30:

> 29 That no flesh should glory in his presence. 30 But of him are ye in Christ Jesus, who of [by] God is made unto us wisdom, and righteousness, and sanctification, and redemption:

As a Pharisee, Paul is very knowledgeable in the Old Testament. He summarizes this by referring to a prophecy. Jeremiah 9:24:

> 24 But let him that glorieth glory in this, that he understandeth
> and knoweth me,
> that I am the LORD which exercise

lovingkindness, judgment, and
righteousness, in the earth:
for in these things I delight,
saith the LORD.

Glory is due to Him alone Who is worthy of Glory.
Paul concludes with this statement in 1 Corinthians
1:31:

31 That, according as it is written, <u>He</u>
<u>that glorieth, let him glory in the Lord.</u>

3

1 Corinthians 2

When Paul originally came to Corinth, he reminds them he did not come as a great orator but instead as one presenting this simple message from God. 1 Corinthians 2:1:

1 And I, brethren, when I came to you, came not with excellency of speech or of wisdom, declaring unto you the testimony of God.

He desired to make known to them only one thing. Verse 2:

2 For I determined not to know any thing among you, save [except] Jesus Christ, and him crucified.

When he arrived in Corinth, he had been chased out

of his previous stop and he was pursued by those who opposed him. The Corinthians were aware of this as he had not hidden it from them. Verses 3-4:

> 3 And I was with you in weakness, and in fear, and in much trembling. 4 And my speech and my preaching was not with enticing words of man's wisdom, but in demonstration of the Spirit and of power:

God's strength is made perfect in weakness. (*cf.* 2 Cor. 12:9.) What reason does he give them? Verse 5:

> 5 That your faith should not stand in the wisdom of men, but [instead] in the power of God.

He did not come to teach worldly wisdom. He came to teach Godly wisdom. Verses 6-7:

> 6 Howbeit we speak wisdom among them [those] that are perfect: yet not the wisdom of this world, nor of the princes of this world, that come to nought [nothing]: 7 But we speak the wisdom of God in a mystery, even [that is to say] the hidden wisdom, which God or-dained before the world unto our

glory:

Think about the word *mystery*. It means *something hidden until it is revealed*. The *mystery* to which Paul is referring was only known to God–the Three in One. That was the case until God Himself revealed it to the Apostle Paul. This *mystery* is explained in the following benediction he wrote in Romans 16:25:

> 25 **Now to him that is of power to stablish you <u>according to my gospel</u>, <u>and the preaching of Jesus Christ</u>, <u>according to the revelation of the mystery</u>, <u>which was kept secret since the world began</u>,**

As I write this to you, I had to get up because of a sudden burst of energy. Sometimes, for me, this is overwhelming emotionally. Friend, this is powerful stuff. It is certainly not milk, but meat for mature believers. Take time to think about this.

As we return to 1 Corinthians, we find additional evidence that no one knew about this *mystery*. We see that it was a complete shock to the watchers and holy ones. Paul is speaking about the *powers and principalities,* the *rulers of darkness* who observe everything. Notice why this was a shock to them. Verse 8:

8 Which none of <u>the princes of this world</u> knew: for had they known it, they would not have crucified the Lord of glory[!].

By killing the Son of God they sealed their own fate! Had they known His death was His victory, they never would *have crucified the Lord of glory!*

Most believers think that God's gift is limited to eternal salvation. Friend, there is so much more! God has always been gracious and generous to those who have faith and patiently wait on Him. Isaiah 64:4:

> **4** For since the beginning of the world men have not heard, nor perceived by the ear, neither hath the eye seen, O God, beside thee, what he hath prepared for him that waiteth for him.

Paul uses the above verse to make his point in 1 Corinthians 2:9:

> **9** But as it is written, Eye hath not seen, nor ear heard, neither have entered into the heart of man, the things which God hath prepared for them that love him.

Speaking to those who are saved by grace through faith, he states that the Spirit of God will reveal to the believers *the deep things of God.* Verse 10:

10 **But God hath revealed them [the deep things of God] unto us by his Spirit: for the Spirit searcheth all things, yea, the deep things of God.**

No one knows us better then we know ourselves. This applies to God too. Verses 11-12:

11 **For what man knoweth the things of a man, save [except] the spirit of man which is in him? even [that is to say] so the things of God knoweth no man, but the Spirit of God [does].** 12 <u>**Now we have received,**</u> **not the spirit of the world, but** <u>**the spirit which is of God;**</u> <u>**that we might know the things that are freely given to us of [by] God.**</u>

We received within us the Spirit of God the moment we were saved and bought by the blood of Christ! Then, the Spirit which is within us teaches us *the deep things of God.*

Paul concludes by making a comparison between *the wisdom of man* and *the wisdom of God. This wisdom of God* can only be taught by the Holy Spirit. Verse 13:

> 13 **Which things also we speak, not in the words which man's wisdom teacheth, but which the Holy Ghost teacheth; [and by] comparing spiritual things with spiritual.**

The best way to understand the Bible, if you should get stuck, is to use the Bible to explain the Bible. Those things which are spiritually understood are best explained by spiritual things. He uses the word *foolishness* again because the natural or unsaved man cannot understand *the deep things of God* for, to him, they are *foolishness*. Verse 14:

> 14 **But the natural man receiveth not the things of the Spirit of God: for they are foolishness unto him: neither can he know them, because they are spiritually discerned.**

However, when we were saved, we received the Holy Spirit Who is now our Teacher. He teaches us and gives us understanding. By having His Spirit, we have *the mind of Christ*. Having His righteousness, we cannot be judged. Verse 15:

15 But he that is spiritual [will] judgeth all things, yet he himself is judged of [by] no man.

Being saved, we are spiritual. We will judge or discern spiritual matters. Spiritually, we have the righteousness of Christ and, therefore, cannot be judged or condemned by any man.

Paul ends with this question, "Who has known the mind of the Lord, that he may instruct Him?" Verse 16:

16 For who hath known the mind of the Lord, that he may instruct him? But we have the mind of Christ.

Having received His Spirit, we may now know *the deep things of God.* Why? Those who have been saved by grace through faith have received His Spirit. *We have the mind of Christ!*

4

1 Corinthians 3

One of the best ways to teach something new is to use a comparison. Before someone can learn *the deep things of God,* they must first move from the basic, or milk, to the more advanced, the meat. This is the comparison Paul makes. 1 Corinthians 3:1-2:

> 1 **And I, brethren, could not speak unto you as unto spiritual, but as unto carnal, even [that is to say] as unto babes in Christ.**
>
> 2 <u>**I have fed you with milk, and not with meat:**</u> **for hitherto ye were not able to bear it, neither yet now are ye able.**

He says he taught them as if they were *babes* or *new believers in the faith* and still they are not ready to handle *the deep things of God.*

In the next verse, the word *carnal* refers to *fleshly* or *worldly*. This is not to be confused with his use of the word *meat* which refers to more advanced or *deeper things of God* suitable for only mature believers. Verses 3-4:

> 3 For ye are yet [still] carnal: for whereas there is among you envying, and strife, and divisions, are ye not [acting] carnal, and walk[ing] as men? 4 For while one saith, I am of Paul; and another, I am of Apollos; are ye not carnal?

The Corinthians are arguing over petty stuff even to the point of who is the one teaching them the truths of God. People do this today. When discussing predestination, some will say, "Calvin says . . ." or some other renown preacher.

Paul continues this thought with verse 5:

> 5 Who then is Paul, and who is Apollos, but ministers by whom ye believed, even as the Lord gave to every man?

Regardless of who planted the seeds of the gospel or who watered them, Paul points out that it is God Who *giveth the increase!* Verses 6-7:

6 I have planted, Apollos watered; but God gave the increase. 7 So then neither is he that planteth any thing, neither he that watereth; but <u>God</u> that <u>giveth the increase</u>.

Those who labor among the believers will receive a reward commensurate with their labor. Verse 8:

8 Now he that planteth and he that watereth are one: and every man shall receive his own reward according to his own labour.

Paul continues to speak about laborers in the ministry. He compares them to husbandry which is the caring of livestock or fields of agriculture. Verse 9:

9 For we are labourers together with God: ye are God's husbandry, ye are God's building.

As an example, he calls himself a wise master builder. Having received the blueprints from the Architect, Paul became His master builder. (*cf.* Gal. 3:1-7.) Those who are in the ministry and come after him must build upon the foundation he laid–which is *Christ!* Verse 10:

10 According to the grace of God which is given unto me, as a wise master-builder, I have laid the foundation, and another buildeth thereon. But let every man take heed how he buildeth there-upon.

The words of a hymn rejoice that "the church's one foundation is Jesus Christ her Lord." There is no other foundation except Christ alone. Verse 11:

11 For other foundation can no man lay than that is laid, which is Jesus Christ.

Every laborer who builds upon this foundation will have their work judged. Remember that each believer has the *righteousness of Christ.* They *cannot* be judged. However, the quality of their workmanship *can* and *will* be judged. Therefore, the following has to do with rewards and not salvation. Verses 12-15:

12 Now if any man build upon this foundation gold, silver, precious stones, wood, hay, stubble; **13** Every man's work shall be made manifest [made known]: for the day shall declare it, because it shall be revealed by fire; and the fire shall try every man's work of what sort it is.

14 If any man's work abide which he hath built thereupon, he shall receive a reward. 15 If any man's work shall be burned, he shall suffer loss: but he himself shall be saved; yet so as by fire.

Every believer's work will be tested by fire in the day of judgment. Although any shoddy workmanship will be destroyed, the laborer *himself shall be saved.*

Paul now begins to teach that *the body* of each believer is *the temple of God.* God's Spirit resides within them. We know that upon believing the gospel of our salvation, the Holy Spirit is given to every believer and dwells within them. Paul instructs them on the care of this *temple* or physical body. Verse 16-17:

16 Know ye not that ye are the temple of God, and that the Spirit of God dwelleth in you? 17 If any man defile the temple of God, him shall God destroy; for the temple of God is holy, which temple ye are.

Do not let those who appear to have wisdom deceive you. The test of truth is always God's Word and everything must be measured against it. Let those who are wise in worldly wisdom become unlearned so that they might receive Godly wisdom. I like to say that there are two people who cannot learn. The first is someone who does not want to learn. The second is someone who believes they know everything. Verses 18-20:

> 18 **Let no man deceive himself. If any man among you <u>seemeth to be wise</u> in this world, <u>let him become a fool, that he may be wise</u>. 19 For <u>the wisdom of this world is foolishness with God</u>. For it is written, He taketh the wise in their own craftiness. 20 And again, The Lord knoweth the thoughts of the wise, that they are vain [empty].**

The word *vain* means *empty, worthless or having no substance, value, or importance*. Therefore, following after the wisdom of men is a complete waste of time.

The vanity of men causes them to be self-centered, puffed up, and self-promoting. When you search for a ministry, look at where they place their focus. Is it focused on Christ? Is it focused on the Word of God? Are they building upon the foundation laid by Paul? Christ is the only true foundation! Verse 21:

> 21 **Therefore let no man glory in men.**

For all things are yours;

He applies the above test to those who teach the Gospel of Grace–including himself. Verse 22:

22 Whether Paul, or Apollos, or Cephas, or the world, or life, or death, or things present, or things to come; all are yours;

Believers have been bought. They have been paid for by His blood. We were redeemed which means bought back from sin and death. We are His. We received the Holy Spirit and were spiritually placed *in Christ* to await our physical redemption. We have the mind of Christ. Now, the Spirit will teach us *the deep things of God*. As we learn, we can be confident of our eternal security for we belong to Christ and He belongs to God. Verse 23:

23 And ye are Christ's; and Christ is God's.[!]

5

1 Corinthians 4

In the previous chapter, Paul tells believers it was he who *laid the foundation*. No one can lay any other foundation. The only foundation is based upon the work completed by Jesus Christ. This is upon this foundation that all others who minister must build. He cautions everyone to take heed in what manner they build thereon. Every laborer is to account or be held responsible for their work. 1 Corinthians 4:1:

> 1 **Let a man so account of us, as of the ministers of Christ, and stewards of the mysteries of God.**

How would someone who is given charge or responsibility of an important job be judged? Paul makes a comparison to a steward who is entrusted with the care of something. It is not the judgment of others that matters. It only depends on the faithfulness of the steward who was entrusted. In the legal world there is a high level of duty in the agent-principal relationship. The duty of the agent to his principal cannot be undermined. Such is the relationship of those who teach and preach the Gospel of Grace. Paul uses the word *stewards* because they *hold something of great value which was given into their care.* Verses 2-4:

> 2 **Moreover it is required in stewards, that a man be found faithful. 3 But with me it is a very small thing that I should be judged of you, or of man's judgment: yea, I judge not mine own self.**

> 4 **For I know nothing by myself; yet am I not hereby justified: but he that judgeth me is the Lord.**

Each steward will be judged by the Lord according to the faithfulness of his stewardship.

Each believer receives the knowledge of the *mystery.* We are to concern ourselves with only our own work; not that of other believers. Every believer will have their work revealed in due time. Verse 5:

> 5 **Therefore judge nothing before the**

time, until the Lord come, who both will bring to light the hidden things of darkness, and will make manifest the counsels of the hearts: and then shall every man have praise of God.

Having this knowledge, do we keep it to ourselves or do we share it with as many people as possible? This sounds a lot like Jesus' parable of the talents. Each of three were given talents. One returned much, one returned a modest amount, and one buried his talent and returned nothing. (*cf.* Matt. 25:14-30.) These stewards, under the Kingdom Gospel, could suffer spiritual loss. Paul is addressing grace believers and there can never be a loss of salvation. Instead, he is dealing with the gain or loss of rewards because, under grace, salvation is not based upon works.

Both Apollos and Paul are just men serving Christ. They are stewards as they teach the good news and build upon His foundation. They are nothing. For everything is about Christ Who is all in all. Verse 6:

6 **And these things, brethren, I have in a figure transferred to myself and to Apollos for your sakes; that ye might learn in us [from our example] not to**

think of men above that which is written, that no one of you be puffed up for one against another.

Some believers, once saved, become proud and boastful in their knowledge of the mystery. Being *puffed up* with egos is unbecoming of anyone saved by grace. For, if it is not by the believer's own works, then what reason has any believer to boast? Verse 7:

> 7 **For who maketh thee to differ from another? and what hast thou that thou didst not receive? now if thou didst receive it, why dost thou glory, as if thou hadst not received it?**

All believers are the same. Each has received salvation as a gift. Therefore, if salvation is a gift, then what is there for any believer to glory or boast in? It was received as a gift and not earned.

There were some believers in Corinth who acted *puffed up.* Paul continues to address them saying that they reign as kings in a prideful way. That will happen someday and Paul looks forward to it. Verse 8:

> 8 **Now ye are full, now ye are rich, ye have reigned as kings without us: and**

**I would [pray] to God ye did reign, that
we also might reign with you.**

He believes God made the apostles to remain last in
this life. They are to be a spectacle and ridiculed before men and the heavenly host. Verse 9:

**9 For I think that God hath set forth us
the apostles last, as it were appointed to
death: for we are made a spectacle unto
the world, and to angels, and to men.**

The apostles are seen as fools, weak, and despised by the world. Yet those in the Corinthian assembly are seen as wise, strong, and honorable.
Verse 10:

**10 We are fools for Christ's sake, but ye
are wise in Christ; we are weak, but ye
are strong; ye are honourable, but we
are despised.**

He writes of the reality of the apostle's circumstances. They are presently suffering in their work
for Christ. Verses 11-13:

**11 Even unto this present hour we both
hunger, and thirst, and are naked, and
are buffeted, and have no certain dwell-**

ing place; 12 And [we] labour, working with our own hands: being reviled, we bless; being persecuted, we suffer it: 13 Being defamed, we intreat: we are made as the filth of the world, and are the off-scouring of all things unto this day.

Notice the reaction of the apostles to each of the degradations they experience. They suffer but their eyes remain focused on the prize–the Lord Jesus Christ.

He tells the Corinthians the truth not to embarrass them but to warn his children in the faith. Verse 15:

14 I write not these things to shame you, but as my beloved sons I warn you.

Although they have many teachers or instructors, like Timothy and Titus, they have one father in the faith. It is through Paul they received the Gospel of Grace and were saved. Verse 15:

15 For though ye have ten thousand instructors in Christ, yet have ye not many fathers: for in Christ Jesus I have begotten you through the gospel.

Having this unique role or position of father in

the faith, Paul beseeches or begs them to be followers of him. Verse 16:

> 16 **Wherefore I beseech you, <u>be ye fol-
> lowers of me.</u>**

Doctrinally, this could be a problem for some Christians who believe they should follow Christ. However, we are told in Scripture that Paul is to be our *pattern* or *example* to follow. Let us stop for a moment. We need to see what Paul wrote to Timothy, another son in the faith, concerning his being a *pattern*. 1 Timothy 1:15-16:

> 15 **This is a faithful saying, and worthy of all acceptation, that <u>Christ Jesus came into the world to save sinners; of whom I am chief.</u>**
>
> 16 **Howbeit for this cause [reason] I obtained mercy, <u>that in me [Paul] first Jesus Christ might shew forth all longsuffering, for a pattern to them which should hereafter believe on him to life everlasting.</u>**

All grace believers are to follow Paul's *pattern* or *example* in the same manner in which *he* follows Christ. The rules for following Christ are different under grace than they were under the Law. They must not be confused. We are not following Paul. We are following his example of the way and manner in which he follows Christ. There is a difference.

Knowing that Timothy understands this, Paul sends him to the assembly in Corinth. Timothy will remind them of Paul's teaching. Through his letters, Paul is able to teach everywhere. Verses 17-18:

> **17 For this cause have I sent unto you Timotheus, who is my beloved son, and faithful in the Lord, who shall bring you into remembrance of my ways which be in Christ, as I teach every where in every church. 18 Now some are puffed up, as though I would not come to you.**

There will always be people who want to assume authority or control over a group. It is human nature. Some did this in Corinth. They thought that Paul would not return and they had the freedom to assert their own teaching. Paul sends Timothy who will not only correct any doctrinal errors, but also advise Paul of the health in the assembly.

However, Paul does intend to come to them, Lord willing. A common title might be *blowhard*. This is someone who is pompous, boastful, and makes a lot of words. Notice what Paul says of these people in verses 19-20:

> 19 **But I will come to you shortly, if the Lord will, and will know, not the speech of them which are puffed up, but the power. 20 For the kingdom of God is not in word [speech], but in power.**

He ends by asking them a question: "So, how do you want it?" It is his intention to come to Corinth to see the believers there. He wants them to be thinking about this. In what manner should he come to them? Should he come to discipline them or to love them in fellowship? Verse 21:

> 21 **What will ye? shall I come unto you with a rod, or in love, and in the spirit of meekness?**

6

1 Corinthians 5

There are other problems within the assembly at Corinth including sexual promiscuity. Not only was it present, but it was being tolerated or ignored by other believers in the assembly. Paul uses the broad term of *fornication* which includes adultery, prostitution, lewdness, incest, and worshipping idols in 1 Corinthians 5:1:

> 1 **It is reported commonly that there is fornication among you, and such fornication as is not so much as named among the Gentiles, that one should have his father's wife.**

This is a sin not even common among the Gentiles. He speaks about one specific member who was involved with his father's wife. This could be either his mother or stepmother, but she was apparently still married to his father. Not only was this known, but they allowed him to remain in the assembly. Verse 2:

> 2 And ye are puffed up, and have not rather mourned, that he that [who] hath done this deed might be taken away from among you.

Paul was able to maintain a connection with the various assemblies by letter. News from the various assemblies was brought by carriers. So, even though he was not able to be with them *in body*, he was with them *in spirit*. As such, he judged this individual. Verse 3:

> 3 For I verily [truly], as absent in body, but present in spirit, have judged already, as though I were present, concerning him that hath so done this deed,

He exercises his apostolic authority as Apostle to the Gentiles. He directs them, when they gather together, to remove him from the assembly. Verses 4-5:

> 4 In the name of our Lord Jesus Christ,

when ye are gathered together, and my spirit, with the power of our Lord Jesus Christ,

5 To deliver such an one unto Satan <u>for the destruction of the flesh</u>, <u>that the spirit may be saved in the day of the Lord Jesus.</u>

By ignoring this sin, they were, in effect, *approving* or *glorying* in it. There is an old saying: a bad apple must be removed to prevent it from spoiling the other good apples. Sin is like yeast being added to dough. It permeates the whole lump of dough. Verses 6-7:

6 Your glorying [approving of this] is not good. Know ye not that a little leaven [yeast] leaveneth the whole lump?

7 Purge out therefore the old leaven, that ye may be a new lump, as ye are unleavened. For even [that is to say] Christ our passover is sacrificed for us:

Leaven or *yeast* was used in the Old Testament to represent sin. Before the Passover, the Law required all Jews to clean their homes and remove all leaven from their households.

The Jews celebrated their first Passover in anticipation of God's delivering them from Egypt. As grace believers, we are to celebrate with joy our deliverance as we await His Calling which is the Rapture. Verse 8:

> 8 **Therefore let us keep the feast, not with old leaven, neither with the leaven of malice and wickedness; but with the unleavened bread of sincerity and truth.**

Believers are not to harbor malice, which means evil, or wickedness. Instead, like unleavened bread, they are to be sincere and share the love of the truth.

Paul tells the believers in Corinth he does not want them to associate with or be in the company of fornicators. To this, he adds others which are similar: coveters, extortioners, or idolators. All of these belong to the world of the children of darkness. Believers are to be the children of light. Verses 9-10:

> 9 **I wrote unto you in an epistle not to [be in the] company with fornicators: 10 Yet not altogether with the fornicators of this world, or with the covetous, or**

extortioners, or with idolaters; for then must ye needs go out of the world.

Often, when Paul is writing an important point in his letters, he will repeat it. Verse 11:

11 But now I have written unto you not to keep company, if any man that is called a brother be a fornicator, or covetous, or an idolater, or a railer, or a drunkard, or an extortioner; with such an one no not to eat.

Someone who *covets* is *envious of what others have.* A person who is a *railer* would be *someone who scoffs, insults, censures or reproaches using disgraceful, shameful, or inflammatory language.* This is not someone you want to sit with at the next covered dish supper.

Many Christians do not want to judge others following Jesus' instruction to "judge not." If judging someone has to do with the unsaved, then I must agree. Judgment is given to Someone far more righteous than we are. However, I believe Paul is talking about *discernment* within the believers. He wants them to recognize evil and to *put away* any wicked and unrepentant person from the assembly. Verses 12-13:

12 For what have I to do to judge them also that are without? do not ye judge them that are within? 13 But them that are without God judgeth. Therefore put away from among yourselves that wicked person.

He is saying that we do not need to judge those who are *without*. These are the unsaved who are outside the fellowship of believers. They are not our concern. He asks the question, "Do not ye judge them that are within?" The unsaved see what those who are inside the fellowship are doing wrong. For the sake of the testimony of believers, *put away from among yourselves that wicked person.*

7

1 Corinthians 6

Wherever two or more are gathered, if they are human, there will be disagreements. Paul gives instruction as to how believers should deal with disagreements. To begin with, believers should not go to the civil courts as they belong to the world. Instead, they must settle the matter within the assembly. 1 Corinthians 6:1:

> 1 **Dare any of you, having a matter against another, go to law before the unjust, and not before the saints?**

He tells the believers about the roles they will play in the future where they are destined to judge the world. Yes, even angels! Verses 2-3:

> 2 **Do ye not know that the saints shall**

judge the world? and if the world shall be judged by you, are ye unworthy to judge the smallest matters? 3 Know ye not that we shall judge angels? how much more things that pertain to this life?

Knowing that believers will deal with such things in the future, they should be able to deal with matters pertaining to other believers in this life. Verse 4:

4 If then ye have judgments of things pertaining to this life, set [appoint] them to judge [those] who are least esteemed in the church.

It would be shameful for grievances to be aired in a public courtroom filled with unbelievers. Therefore, someone within the assembly must be capable of settling disagreements between believers. Verses 5-6:

5 I speak to your shame. Is it so, that there is not a wise man among you? no, not one that shall be able to judge between his brethren? 6 But brother goeth to law [court] with brother, and that before the unbelievers.

Instead of fighting for what someone feels is due them, Paul, in effect, asks a question. "Why not just forgive others as Christ Himself has forgiven you?" This would be *applied* grace or, in other words, grace *in action*. Here is something interesting. Grace is actually the inverse of the Lord's Prayer found in Matthew 6:12:

> 12 **And <u>forgive us our debts, as we forgive our debtors.</u>**

We are no longer in the *Age of Law* but instead are in the *Age of Grace*. We should pray: Lord, help us to forgive others as Christ has already forgiven us. 1 Corinthians 6:7-8:

> 7 **Now therefore there is utterly a fault among you, because ye go to law [the court] one with another. <u>Why do ye not rather take wrong? why do ye not rather suffer yourselves to be defrauded?</u> 8 Nay, ye [also] do wrong, and defraud, and that [to] your brethren.**

As grace believers, we are *the children of light* and God expects us to act graciously towards other believers.

There are certain expectations of those who are *the children of light*. Verses 9-11:

9 Know ye not that the unrighteous shall not inherit the kingdom of God? Be not deceived: neither fornicators, nor idolaters, nor adulterers, nor effeminate, nor abusers of themselves with mankind, 10 Nor thieves, nor covetous, nor drunkards, nor revilers, nor extortioners, shall inherit the kingdom of God.

11 And such were some of you: but ye are washed, but ye are sanctified, but ye are justified in the name of the Lord Jesus, and by the Spirit of our God.

For *the children of light* have been proclaimed justified by the washing of His blood. They are being sanctified by the Holy Spirit to be conformed to His image. Finally, we are awaiting the redemption of our body at *His Calling.* Maybe, knowing all this, we should play nice with the other kids in the grace sandbox-assembly.

Being *under grace* is completely different than being *under the Law.* Paul explains the purpose of the Law. It was to bring everyone to the conclusion that all have sinned and fallen short of the requirements of the Law. Galatians 3:21-26:

21 Is the law then against the promises

of God? God forbid: for if there had been a law given which could have given life, <u>verily righteousness should have been by the law.</u>

22 <u>But the scripture hath concluded all under sin, that the promise by faith of Jesus Christ might be given to them that believe.</u>

23 But <u>before faith</u> came, <u>we were kept under the law,</u> shut up unto the faith which should afterwards be revealed. 24 Wherefore <u>the law was our schoolmaster to bring us unto Christ, that we might be justified by faith.</u> 25 But after that faith is come, we are no longer under a schoolmaster. [Why?]

26 For ye are all the children of God by faith in Christ Jesus[!].

Once we receive salvation as a gift of God by faith, we must add nothing. Having received *liberty*, which is freedom from the Law, we must not fall under its *yoke of bondage* again. Galatians 5:1:

1 <u>Stand fast therefore in the liberty wherewith Christ hath made us free,</u>

and be <u>not entangled again with the yoke of bondage.</u>

Knowing this, we can now read and understand the following. 1 Corinthians 6:12:

> 12 **All things are lawful unto me, but all things are not expedient: all things are lawful for me, but I will not be brought under the power of any.**

Paul gives an example. Meat or food is made for the belly. Food is to be eaten and digested. The belly is made for food so that it can be digested to nourish the body. Both of these are temporary and for use only while we are in our present body. Someday, our old body will pass away and we will receive our glorified body at *His Calling*. Verses 13-14:

> 13 **Meats for the belly, and the belly for meats: but God shall destroy both it and them. Now the body is not for fornication, but for the Lord; and the Lord for the body. 14 And God hath both raised up the Lord, and will also raise up us by his own power.**

We must remind ourselves that our earthly bodies are temporary. They are for use only while we remain here on earth waiting for our bodily redemption.

Paul uses the body to compare our bodies to being a *member* of the Body of Christ. Here, a *member* would include His hands, arms, and feet. Therefore, how these *members* are used should be acceptable and honoring to Christ. Verses 15-17:

> 15 Know ye not that <u>your bodies are the members of Christ</u>? shall I then take the members of Christ, and make them the members of an harlot? God forbid.
>
> 16 What? know ye not that he which is joined to an harlot is one body? for two, saith he, shall be one flesh. 17 But he that is joined unto the Lord is one spirit.

How and with whom we use our bodies is important knowing that it is with the Lord we are joined together by one Spirit.

What then is a believer to do? Paul gives instructions in verse 18:

> 18 Flee fornication. Every sin that a man doeth is without the body; but he that committeth fornication sinneth against

his own body.

For our body is the dwelling place of the Holy Spirit. It is a tabernacle or temple in which the Spirit resides. We have been bought with His blood and belong to Him. We are no longer our own. Verse 19:

> 19 **What? know ye not that your body is the temple of the Holy Ghost which is in you, which ye have of God, and ye are not your own?**

Paul concludes by reminding the Corinthians of something none of us should forget. Verse 20:

> 20 **For <u>ye are bought with a price</u>: therefore glorify God in your body, and in your spirit, which are God's.**

8

1 Corinthians 7

Letters are sent from Paul to the other assemblies while news is generally received by reports from travelers. Of all his letters, some wonder why there are not more of his letters included in the Bible. Remember that the Bible tells us what God wants us to know and not necessarily everything we want to know. The Bible is the work of the Holy Spirit. The letters in Scripture are the ones the Spirit chose to include. They serve His purpose. Furthermore, the Spirit preserves them for us in the Word of God. God makes a promise concerning His Word in Psalms 12:6-7:

> 6 **The words of the LORD are pure words: as silver tried in a furnace of earth, purified seven times. 7 Thou shalt keep them, O LORD, thou shalt pre-**

**serve them from this generation for
ever.**

People have told me that much of what Paul
writes is his own personal opinion. It may be that his
"opinions" offend them. It is written that "all scripture is given by inspiration of God . . ." (2 Tim. 3:16).
Unless he specifically states it is his own opinion,
which he does on occasion, his words are inspired.
Even when Paul gives his own opinion, as the Apostle to the Gentiles, it may not be a commandment of
God, it is written with His approval.

Some of his subjects are surprisingly candid. It
is for that reason, Pauline doctrine is meat and not
milk. In other words, his teachings are for those who
are mature in Christ. He deals with all sorts of topics.
1 Corinthians 7:1:

> 1 **Now concerning the things whereof ye
> wrote unto me: It is good for a man not
> to touch a woman.**

Here, Paul responds to a question about abstinence
in the marriage. He begins by defining the marriage
relationship. Believers must avoid *fornication* which
is *the sexual union between unmarried partners*. Therefore, sexual relations must be restricted to the marriage. Verses 2-3:

64

2 Nevertheless, to avoid fornication, let every man have his own wife, and let every woman have her own husband. 3 Let the husband render unto the wife due benevolence: and likewise also the wife unto the husband.

Both the husband and wife should show *benevolence,* which are *acts of kindness and love,* toward each other.

The next verse needs to be prefaced with this comment. Paul is not addressing *women* in general. but is speaking specifically about a *wife.* A *wife* is a married *woman* who is under a covenant agreement. So too is her husband. He is a *man* who is married. If someone is looking to blame someone, then they must not blame Paul. For it is God Who made this happen six thousand years ago when He created the first man and woman. Genesis 2:21-23:

21 And the LORD God caused a deep sleep to fall upon Adam, and he slept: and he took one of his ribs, and closed up the flesh instead thereof;

22 And the rib, which the LORD God had taken from man, made he a woman, and brought her unto the man.

23 And Adam said, <u>This is now bone of my bones, and flesh of my flesh: she shall be called Woman, because she was taken out of Man</u>.

To follow is the verse read at many marriage ceremonies to commemorate the first marriage union. Verse 24:

24 Therefore shall a man leave his father and his mother, and shall cleave unto his wife: <u>and they shall be one flesh</u>.

This last verse gives us *God's* view of marriage. Marriage is between one man and one woman *and they shall be one flesh.*

From this viewpoint, Paul continues writing about the *husband and wife.* 1 Corinthians 7:4:

4 The wife hath not power of her own body, but the husband: and likewise also the husband hath not power of his own body, but the wife.

Of course each has control of their own body. Paul is saying that they do not have *complete* control. They are no longer a single person; no longer considering only themselves or their own needs. They are now united forming *one flesh.*

In the next verse, Paul uses the words *defraud* in its original meaning. We must not misunderstand his use of this word. Here, the word *defraud* means to *deprive someone of what is rightfully theirs, to wrongfully withhold from someone what is due them,* or *to prevent someone from fully obtaining what is justly their claim.* Understanding this, let us continue with verse 5:

> 5 **Defraud ye not one the other, except it be with consent for a time, that ye may give yourselves to fasting and prayer; and come together again, that Satan tempt you not for your incontinency.**

Paul is discussing sexual union. Neither one should *defraud* or *prevent the other from obtaining what is justly their claim or what is rightfully theirs.* This is the cement that holds the two together. Why does Paul say this? It is because Satan may use this for temptation because the sexual desire can be very powerful. We must remember that it is God-given. It is for procreation as well as intimacy between the *husband and wife.* The word *incontinency* means *the inability to restrain.* Applied to this subject, he is referring to the restraint of passions or appetites leading to an uncontrolled indulgence of them.

Sometimes, Paul does express his own opinions. God gives him permission to do so and he informs the reader. Such is the case here. Verses 7:6-7:

> 6 But [Except] I speak this by permission, and not of commandment. 7 For I would [desire] that all men were even as I [am] myself. But every man hath his proper gift of God, one after this manner, and another after that.

Paul is single. He knows that married men are not free to do as they wish because they are in a partnership. For those in ministry, he desires that they remain, like himself, single. Then, he concludes that this matter is different for each man to decide according to God's will for them.

It must not be misconstrued that Paul is against marriage. However, for the unmarried and widowed, he makes this suggestion. They should think and pray about the ramifications of such a commitment before making it. Verses 8-9:

> 8 I say therefore to the unmarried and widows, It is good for them if they abide [remain single] even as I. 9 But if they cannot contain, let them marry: for it is better to marry than to burn.

Using the word *contain,* he returns to the idea of *incontinency.* For those who cannot *contain* their passion, it is better for them to marry than to fall into sin. This has nothing to do with salvation, He reminds them that sin has earthly consequences.

He writes to those in the assembly who are married. No longer giving his opinion, but now speaking for the Lord. This is clear from his words: *yet not I, but the Lord* in verses 10-11:

> 10 **And unto the married I command, yet not I, but the Lord, Let not the wife depart from her husband: 11 But and if she depart, let her remain unmarried, or be reconciled to her husband: and let not the husband put away his wife.**

Again, the above is not his own opinion but a commandment from the Lord. Then, he gives his opinion in verses 12-13:

> 12 **But to the rest speak I, not the Lord: If any brother hath a wife that believeth not, and she be pleased to dwell with him, let him not put her away. 13 And the woman which hath an husband that believeth not, and if he be pleased to dwell with her, let her not leave him.**

These two situations are the same. One marriage partner is saved while the other is not. If the unbeliever is pleased to dwell with the believer, then they should continue in their marriage.

Paul explains why in verses 14-15:

14 For the unbelieving husband is sanctified by the [believing] wife, and the unbelieving wife is sanctified by the [believing] husband: else [otherwise] were your children unclean; but now are they holy.

15 But if the unbelieving depart, let him depart. A brother or a sister is not under bondage in such cases: but God hath called us to peace.

Paul concludes by saying that the saved partner, by their example, may lead the unsaved partner to salvation. Verse 16:

16 For what knowest thou, O wife, whether thou shalt save thy husband? or how knowest thou, O man, whether thou shalt save thy wife?

In whatever situation a person finds themselves when they were saved, they should continue in it and be content therein. Here, Paul is not speaking about a state of sinfulness but rather the individual's station or circumstance. Verses 17-24:

> 17 **But as God hath distributed to every man, as the Lord hath called every one, so let him walk. And so ordain I in all churches. 18 Is any man called being circumcised? let him not become uncircumcised. Is any called in uncircumcision? let him not be circumcised. 19 Circumcision is nothing, and uncircumcision is nothing, but the keeping of the commandments of God.**
>
> 20 **Let every man abide in the same calling wherein he was called. 21 Art thou called being a servant? care not for it: but if thou mayest be made free, use it rather. 22 For he that is called in the Lord, being a servant, is the Lord's freeman: likewise also he that is called, being free, is Christ's servant.**
>
> 23 **Ye are bought with a price; be not ye the servants of men. 24 Brethren, let every man, wherein [from whatever] he is called, therein abide with God.**

In the following verses, he uses the phrase *I have no commandment of the Lord: yet I give my judgment*. This implies he is making his own personal observation. Verses 25-28:

> 25 **Now concerning virgins I have no commandment of the Lord: yet I give my judgment, as one that hath obtained mercy of the Lord to be faithful.**
>
> 26 **I suppose therefore that this is good for the present distress, I say, that it is good for a man so to be. 27 Art thou bound unto a wife? seek not to be loosed. Art thou loosed from a wife? seek not a wife.**
>
> 28 **But and if thou marry, thou hast not sinned; and if a virgin marry, she hath not sinned. Nevertheless such shall have trouble in the flesh: but I spare you.**

He uses the word *spare* meaning he will *spare* them further elaboration on this subject.

Paul, still speaking in the first person, continues with his own opinion saying *the time is short*. This is exactly how many believers feel today. He is concerned about their state of mind. Verses 29-31:

> 29 But this I say, brethren, the time is short: it [what little time] remaineth, that both they that have wives be as though they had none; 30 And they that weep, as though they wept not; and they that rejoice, as though they rejoiced not; and they that buy, as though they possessed not; 31 And they that use this world, as not abusing it: for the fashion of this world passeth away.

Grace believers should not be consumed with their current state since such little time remains. Our time here on earth is short. *His Calling* or *the Rapture* is imminent.

Paul uses the word *carefulness* to mean *the state of being full of care or anxious.* He does not want their lives to be filled with cares or anxiety. He uses the word *careth* four times in verses 32-35:

> 32 But I would [desire to] have you without carefulness [anxiety]. He that is unmarried <u>careth</u> for the things that belong to the Lord, how he may please the Lord: 33 But he that is married <u>careth</u> for the things that are of the world, how he

may please his wife. 34 **There is [a] difference also between a wife and a virgin. The unmarried woman** <u>careth</u> **for the things of the Lord, that she may be holy both in body and in spirit: but she that is married** <u>careth</u> **for the things of the world, how she may please her husband.**

35 **And this I speak for your own profit; not that I may cast a snare upon you, but for that which is comely [fit or suitable], and that ye may attend upon [serve] the Lord without distraction.**

Paul's purpose is to encourage believers to focus on the work of the Lord. As grace believers, Paul explains our purpose or mission for the time remaining.

As believers saved by grace, we have a sacred task! We are to make known the Gospel of Grace to others who are not saved so that they too may be reconciled to God. For those who are *called according to His purpose,* you might ask what is God's purpose or ultimate desire? We are told in 1 Timothy 2:3-4:

3 **For this is good and acceptable in the sight of God our Saviour;** 4 <u>**Who will**</u>

have all men to be saved, and to come unto the knowledge of the truth.

Each one who is saved by grace through faith has heard the Gospel of Grace and, by believing it, they were saved. As grace believers, we must share this simple message of salvation. Paul writes about this in Romans 10:17:

> 17 **So then faith cometh by hearing, and hearing by the word of God.**

Therefore, Paul is concerned that believers will be distracted from this duty. Paul writes that every believer is an *ambassador of reconciliation*. 2 Corinthians 5:18-20:

> 18 **And all things are of <u>God</u>, who hath reconciled us to himself by Jesus Christ, and <u>hath given to us the ministry of reconciliation</u>; 19 To wit, that God was in Christ, reconciling the world unto himself, not imputing their trespasses unto them; and [God] <u>hath committed unto us the word of reconciliation</u>.**
>
> 20 **Now then we are <u>ambassadors for Christ</u>, as though God did beseech [implore] you by us: we pray you in**

Christ's stead, be ye reconciled to God.

Grace believers are reconciled to God through the blood of His Son Jesus Christ. Paul does not want anything to deter us from our ministry of sharing the wonderful news of this Gospel of Grace with others!

As you know, those who are married do not have full control of their own lives. The needs of their partner will reduce the time and energy put into this ministry. The next verse requires a definition. The word *comely* means *that which is becoming, fit, or suitable in its form or manner.* Let us return to 1 Corinthians 7:36:

> 36 But if any man think that he behaveth himself uncomely toward his virgin, if she pass the flower of her age, and need so require, let him do what he will [choose], he sinneth not: let them marry.

If a man or woman chooses to marry, then let them marry. Verses 37-38:

> 37 Nevertheless he that standeth stedfast in his heart, having no necessity [need], but hath power over his own will, and hath so decreed in his heart that he will keep his virgin [state], [then he] doeth

well. **38 So then he that giveth her in marriage [marries] doeth well; but he that giveth her not in marriage [does not marry] doeth better.**

For the furtherance of the ministry, Paul states that the one who does not marry does better.

Paul concludes by discussing divorce in verses 39-40:

39 The wife is bound by the law as long as her husband liveth; but if her husband be dead, she is at liberty to be married to whom she will; only in the Lord.

40 But she is happier if she so abide, after my judgment: and I think also that I have the Spirit of God.

A saved widow is free to marry again, but only to a man who is also saved. However, in Paul's opinion, it is best if she also remains single. In this matter, he believes, the Spirit of God agrees.

9

1 Corinthians 8

Corinth is a city filled with unsaved Gentiles who worship idols. Therefore, it is part of their culture. Naturally, living in this environment, believers need instruction on how to deal with certain issues. 1 Corinthians 8:1:

> 1 **Now as touching [concerning] things offered unto idols, we know that we all have knowledge. Knowledge puffeth up, but charity edifieth.**

When the Bible speaks about knowledge and wisdom, knowledge is usually of man and wisdom is usually of God. So, the knowledge of man puffs up the ego while charity, or love, lifts up. Verses 2-3:

> 2 **And if any man think that he knoweth**

any thing, he knoweth nothing yet [except] as he ought to know. 3 But if any man love God, the same is known of him.

People notice. Those who act haughty in their knowledge, beyond what he should know, are seen. Additionally, those who love God and show it in their actions are known by them as well.

At this time, people might barter for services instead of using money. Since idols require sacrifices, often times, these offerings are made with meats or produce. Later, these offerings could be sold by the respective temples. This resulted in an ethical problem for the Corinthians believers. Verses 4-6:

4 As concerning therefore the eating of those things that are offered in sacrifice unto idols, we know that an idol is nothing in the world, and that there is none other God but one.

5 For though there be that are called gods, whether in heaven or in earth, (as there be gods many, and lords many,)

6 But to us there is but one God, the Father, of whom are all things, and we in

him; and one Lord Jesus Christ, by whom are all things, and we by him.

There are no other gods except the One Who created heaven and earth. Therefore, these idols are nothing.

Not everyone has this knowledge. For that reason, Paul includes these instructions. Some do not realize that idols are nothing. When they eat food offered to idols, their conscience causes them to experience guilt and they think their body is now defiled Verse 7.

7 Howbeit there is not in every man that knowledge [understanding]: for some with conscience of the idol unto this hour eat it as a thing offered unto an idol; and their conscience being weak is defiled.

The word *commendeth* means *to make acceptable or more acceptable.* Verse 8:

8 But meat commendeth us not to God: for neither, if we eat, are we the better; neither, if we eat not, are we the worse.

So, whether they eat or do not eat the food, believers are neither the better not worse for it. In other words, there is no effect!

However, Paul offers this caution to the mature believers. It concerns those who are weaker or new in the faith. Verse 9:

9 But take heed lest by any means this liberty of yours become a stumbling-block to them that are weak.

Much of what is learned in the assembly is done by teaching, but also by observation of those who have been taught. This may be a funny saying, but it is true: monkey see; monkey do. Weaker believers in the faith learn from the example of those who are mature. Mature believers should be aware of this. Verses 10-11:

10 For if any man see thee which hast knowledge [who is mature] sit at meat in the idol's temple, shall not the conscience of him which is weak be emboldened to eat those things which are offered to idols;

11 And through thy knowledge shall the weak brother perish [stumble], for whom Christ died?

Notice that this is by observation only. If a mature believer was to teach or explain the circumstances to the weaker believer, this would not be a problem. With lack of teaching, the freedom of the mature believer may cause spiritual harm to the weaker believer for whom Christ also died.

Whether eating sacrifices to non-existent gods or some other freedom enjoyed by mature believers, they must not offend the new believer in the faith. Any negligence of conscience for this weaker brother or sister is an offense against Christ. Verses 12-13:

> 12 **But when ye sin so against the brethren, and wound their weak conscience, ye sin against Christ.**
>
> 13 **Wherefore, if meat make my brother to offend, I will eat no flesh while the world standeth [publically], lest I make my brother to offend.**

10

1 Corinthians 9

Paul uses a style common to Greek philosophers who begin arguments by posing questions. Then, they proceed to answer their questions. 1 Corinthians 9:1:

> 1 **Am I not an apostle? am I not free? have I not seen Jesus Christ our Lord? are not ye my work in the Lord?**

To each of these four questions, the Corinthians would answer yes. He may not be the apostle to everyone, but he certainly is their apostle. For they are the proof of his apostleship. Verse 2:

> 2 **If I be not an apostle unto others, yet doubtless I am to you: for the seal of mine apostleship are ye in the Lord.**

They are now saved because they heard and believed Paul's gospel. They are the evidence of his apostleship *in Christ!*

Paul's authority is often challenged and here he answers them in verses 3-5:

> 3 **Mine answer to them that do examine me is this,** 4 **Have we not power to eat and to drink?**

> 5 **Have we not power to lead about a sister, a wife, as well as other apostles, and as the brethren of the Lord, and Cephas?**

There is a reason that he is making these statements which we will see in a moment. Since this letter was written at the beginning of his ministry, his traveling associate was Barnabas. Verses 6-7:

> 6 **Or I only and Barnabas, have not we power to forbear working [not work]?**

> 7 **Who goeth a warfare [goes to war] any time at his own charges [expense]? who planteth a vineyard, and eateth not of the fruit thereof? or who feedeth a flock, and eateth not of the milk of the**

flock?

Soldiers are paid to go to war. Farmers who grow produce and those who tend livestock receive the benefits of their work.

He continues by providing additional evidence to support his point. Verses 8-10:

> 8 Say I these things as a man? or saith not the law the same also? 9 For it is written in the law of Moses, Thou shalt not muzzle the mouth of the ox that treadeth out the corn. Doth God take care for oxen?

> 10 Or saith he it altogether for our sakes? For our sakes, no doubt, this is written: that he that ploweth should plow in hope [expectation]; and that he that thresheth [grain] in hope should be partaker of his hope [expectation].

Here, he makes his point to them in verses 11-12:

> 11 If we have sown unto you spiritual things, is it a great thing if we shall reap your carnal things? 12 If others be partakers of this power over you, are

not we rather? <u>Nevertheless we have</u> <u>not used this power; but suffer all</u> <u>things, lest [that by doing so] we should</u> <u>hinder the gospel of Christ.</u>

Having sown spiritual seeds among them, Paul and his companions have a right to receive benefit from them. However, this right is not exercised for one reason. They do not want, in any way, to hinder the advancement of the Gospel of Grace. Therefore, they suffer for the sake of the gospel message that it be hindered by nothing.

The priests and attendants in the temples receive a living from those who worship there. Verses 13-14:

> **13 Do ye not know that they which minister about holy things live of the things of the temple? and they which wait at the altar are partakers with the altar? 14 Even so hath the Lord ordained that they which preach the gospel should live of the gospel.**

He wants them to know that God desires that those who minister in the gospel should receive an income from its followers as well.

Although God's wishes concerning income may apply to others, Paul declines to receive wages from the believers. Verse 15:

15 But I have used none of these things: neither have I written these things, that it should be so done unto me: for it were better for me to die, than that any man should make my glorying void.

He does not want to receive any compensation so *that any man should make my glorying void.* For his work is not done by him, but by Christ Who is in him. Therefore, he preaches the Gospel of Grace without cost.

He does not want anyone to say that they *paid* Paul to receive the gospel. He makes it clear that he wants to glorify Christ. Verse 16:

16 For though I preach the gospel, I have nothing to glory of: for necessity is laid upon me; yea, woe is unto me, if I preach not the gospel!

Paul is compelled by the Spirit within him to preach the gospel. The responsibility has been given to him. He is the Apostle of the Gospel of the Grace of God. Verses 17-18:

17 For if I do this thing willingly, I have a reward: but if against my will, a dispensation of the gospel is committed unto me.

18 What is my reward then? Verily [Truly] that, <u>when I preach the gospel, I may make the gospel of Christ without charge</u>, that I abuse not my power in the gospel.

He does not want to profit by the gospel. Many world evangelists cannot say that.

Paul voluntarily makes himself a servant to all. By doing so, his heavenly reward will be far greater. Verse 19:

19 For though I be free from all men, yet have I made myself servant unto all, that I might gain [reach] the more [of them].

Paul becomes whatever is necessary to reach different people. He lists some examples in verses 20-22:

20 And unto the Jews I became as a Jew, that I might gain the Jews; to them that are under the law, as under the law,

that I might gain them that are under the law;

21 To them that are without law, as without law, (being not without law to God, but under the law to Christ,) that I might gain them that are without law.

22 To the weak became I as weak, that I might gain the weak: I am made all things to all men, that I might by all means save some.

Why does he do this? Verse 23:

23 And this I do for the gospel's sake, that I might be partaker thereof with you.

All of those who participate in a race are there to run. Each runner strives to obtain the prize or, at the least, to finish the race. Verse 24:

24 Know ye not that they which run in a race run all, but [only] one receiveth the prize? So run, that ye [you all] may obtain [the prize].

Below, the word *temperate* means to be *moderate and*

without excess. It is Paul's desire to remain *temperate in all things.* Verse 25:

> 25 And every man that striveth [in the race] for the mastery is temperate in all things. Now they do it to obtain a corruptible crown; but we [do it to obtain] an incorruptible [crown].

Paul is speaking about the work of the gospel of grace. Those who run a race look for an earthly prize which is corruptible. However, grace believers who share the gospel seek a heavenly *reward* which is an *incorruptible crown.* This crown which we will receive at *His Calling* is incorruptible and eternal.

Paul seeks to keep his body under control by keeping his flesh in subjection to Christ. He does this so that his preaching of the gospel to others will not be tarnished. His failure to keep his own flesh in subjection might cause him to lose his heavenly reward. Verses 26-27:

> 26 I therefore so run, not as uncertainly; so fight I, not as one that beateth the air: 27 But I keep under my body, and bring it into subjection: lest that by any means, when I have preached to others, I myself should be a castaway.

Paul is certainly confident of his eternal salvation. Since he is speaking of works, the only loss he could suffer would be his loss of rewards. Rewards will be received on *the day of the Lord Jesus Christ.* This is also known as *His Calling* or the Rapture. He wants the Corinthians and, for that matter, all grace believers to receive their rewards in Christ. Remember Paul's words in 1 Corinthians 1:6-9:

> 6 **Even as the testimony of Christ was confirmed [made sure] in you: 7 So that ye come behind [lack] in no gift [reward]; waiting for <u>the coming of our Lord Jesus Christ</u>:**
>
> 8 **Who shall also confirm you [your salvation] unto the end, that ye may be blameless in <u>the day of our Lord Jesus Christ</u>.**
>
> 9 **God is faithful, by whom ye were called unto the fellowship of his Son Jesus Christ our Lord.[!]**

11

1 Corinthians 10

At the beginning of his ministry, Paul would go to the Jews first and also to the Greeks. (*cf.* Rom. 1:16, 2:10.) It is for this reason he makes frequent references to Jewish history. He says that he does not want them to be unaware or unaware of certain facts. 1 Corinthians 10:1:

> 1 **Moreover, brethren, I would not that ye should be ignorant, how that all our fathers were under the cloud, and all passed through the sea;**

Not only did Israel pass through the Red Sea, they stood under a cloud that followed them. God provided them with manna, food from heaven. They all drank from the water that flowed from the Rock which followed them as well. Verses 2-4:

2 And were all baptized unto Moses in the cloud and in the sea; 3 And did all eat the same spiritual meat [food];

4 And did all drink the same spiritual drink: for they drank of that spiritual Rock that followed them: and that Rock was Christ.

The rock from which the Israelites received their water in the desert was Christ. This Rock would supply the water from which they all could drink.

In spite of these abundant provisions which they received from the hand of God, many chose not to please Him. Verse 5:

5 But with many of them God was not well pleased: for they were overthrown in the wilderness.

They rebelled against God their Provider. It was their disobedience and lack of faith in a faithful God that resulted in their wandering in the Wilderness for forty years. Paul says their historic failures are to be examples to all the faithful. Verses 6-8:

6 Now these things were our examples, to the intent we should not lust after

evil things, as they also lusted. 7 Neither be ye idolaters, as were some of them; as it is written, The people sat down to eat and drink, and rose up to play.

8 Neither let us commit fornication, as some of them committed, and fell in one day three and twenty thousand.

He warns the Corinthians not to test God. Learn from these examples. He continues with verses 9-10:

9 Neither let us tempt [test] Christ, as some of them also tempted [tested God], and were destroyed of [by] serpents.

10 Neither murmur [grumble or complain] ye, as some of them also murmured [grumbled or complained], and were destroyed of [by] the destroyer.

All of these things happened to Israel that they may be teaching examples to both them as well as to those saved by grace. Verse 11:

11 Now all these things happened unto them for ensamples [examples]: and

they are written for our admonition, upon whom the ends of the world are come.

Israel was tested and failed. He warns that no one should be overly self-confident. If they do, then they should *take heed* or *pay attention* so that they do not fall. Verse 12:

12 **Wherefore let him that thinketh he standeth take heed lest he fall.**

There is good news for believers. God will not test us beyond our ability to withstand it. He always provides a way of escape and we have His Word on this. Verse 13:

13 **There hath no temptation [testing] taken [put upon] you but such as is common to man: but God is faithful, who will not suffer [allow] you to be tempted [tested] above that ye are able; but will with the temptation [testing] also make a way to escape, that ye may be able to bear it.**

The process of sanctification is separating us from what is worldly. In other words, if believers are to be holy unto God, then they must turn away from everything that is worldly or evil. This is important. Paul wants all believers to pay attention to this. Verses 14-15:

> 14 **Wherefore, my dearly beloved, flee from idolatry. 15 I speak as to wise men; judge ye what I say.**

He is speaking to those who should understand and, therefore, make wise judgments.

Communion is representative of the fellowship and oneness of believers. All believers are one in Christ: in His blood and in His body. Verses 16-17:

> 16 **The cup of blessing which we bless, is it not the communion of the blood of Christ? The bread which we break, is it not the communion of the body of Christ? 17 For we being many are one bread, and one body: for we are all partakers of that one bread.**

He compares this to the communion between Israel and God. Verse 18:

> 18 **Behold Israel after the flesh: are not they which eat of the sacrifices partakers of the altar?**

There is only one God. Therefore, idols are nothing. However, worshippers who sacrifice to idols are actually in communion with principalities, powers, and rulers of the darkness of this world. (*cf.* Eph. 6:12.) From this evil we are to separate ourselves. Verses 19-22:

> 19 **What say I then? that the idol is any thing, or that which is offered in sacrifice to idols is any thing?**
>
> 20 **But I say, that the things which the Gentiles sacrifice, they sacrifice to devils, and not to God: and I would not that ye should have fellowship [communion] with devils.**
>
> 21 **Ye cannot drink the cup of the Lord, and the cup of devils: ye cannot be partakers of the Lord's table, and of the table of devils.** 22 **Do we provoke the Lord to jealousy? are we stronger than he?**

This can only be understood by mature believers. For believers who are still new in the faith, it will take time. For Paul and mature believers, all things under grace are acceptable. Yet, everything is not necessarily profitable or useful. Neither does everything edify or lift up. Verses 23-24:

23 All things are lawful for me, but all things are not expedient: all things are lawful for me, but all things edify not. **24** Let no man seek his own, but every man another's wealth.

Mature believers must not think only of themselves but consider the weaker brethren who watch them. The word *shambles* means *a flesh-market or the place where butchered meat is sold.* Verses 25-26:

25 Whatsoever is sold in the shambles, that [you may] eat, asking no question for conscience sake: **26** For the earth is the Lord's, and the fulness thereof.

Under grace, the mature believer has liberty to enjoy both the Lord and the fulness of His Creation. If you are invited to a feast and choose to go, eat what is presented without asking questions. Verse 27:

27 If any of them that believe not bid you to a feast, and ye be disposed to go; whatsoever is set before you, eat, asking no question for conscience sake.

Once informed that the meat was offered to idols, for the sake of the weaker believer, the mature believer should refrain from eating it. Verses 28-30:

101

28 But if any man say unto you, This is offered in sacrifice unto idols, eat not for his sake that shewed it, and for conscience sake: for the earth is the Lord's, and the fulness thereof:

29 Conscience, I say, not thine own, but of the other: for why is my liberty judged of another man's conscience?

30 For if I by grace be a partaker, why am I evil spoken of for that for which I give thanks?

It is the conscience of the weaker believers who fear that eating such is sin. It causes them to judge the mature believer who knows that it is acceptable to God. This can be applied to anything. Verses 31-33:

31 Whether therefore ye eat, or drink, or whatsoever ye do, do all to the glory of God. 32 Give none [no one] offence, neither to the Jews, nor to the Gentiles, nor to the church [called-out] of God:

33 Even as I please all men in all things, not seeking mine own profit, but the profit of many, that they may be saved.

As mature believers, we are to not offend anyone. Instead, like Paul, we must first seek the welfare of many concerning their salvation. Paul's foremost concern is God's will have *all men to be saved and to come unto the knowledge of the truth.* 1 Timothy 2:3-4:

> **3 For this is good and acceptable in the sight of God our Saviour;**
>
> **4 <u>Who will have all men to be saved, and to come unto the knowledge of the truth.</u>**

The above verse is proof that God does not preselect those who will be saved and those who will not. He wants everyone to come to the knowledge or understanding of the truth. Then, using their own free will, they can make their decision to accept or reject it.

12

1 Corinthians 11

God made Paul to be a pattern for those believers who come after him. He is to be their example. (*cf.* 1 Tim. 1:16.) Therefore, all grace believers are to follow Paul, in like manner, as he himself follows Christ. 1 Corinthians 11:1:

> 1 **Be ye followers of me, even [that is to say] as I also am of Christ.**

He commends the believers who remember his teaching and did not change it. They held true to the doctrine as he originally presented it to them. Verse 2:

> 2 **Now I praise you, brethren, that ye remember me in all things, and keep the ordinances [teaching], as I delivered them to you.**

He begins to teach about man and woman. Verse 3:

> 3 But I would have you know, that the head of every man is Christ; and the head of the woman is the man; and the head of Christ is God.

With greater responsibility also comes greater accountability.

Paul lays out a hierarchal order of responsibility which has held true since the days of the patriarchs. This could be highly offensive in today's society. One must realize that Corinthians was written to many Jewish believers during Paul's earlier ministry. However, rather than objecting, we must try to understand Paul's teaching. Verses 4-7:

> 4 Every man praying or prophesying, having his head covered, dishonoureth his head. 5 But every woman that prayeth or prophesieth with her head uncovered dishonoureth her head: for that is even all one [the same] as if she were shaven.
>
> 6 For if the woman be not covered, let her also be shorn: but if it be a shame for a woman to be shorn or shaven, let

her be covered.

7 For a man indeed ought not to cover his head, forasmuch as he is the image and glory of God: but the woman is the glory of the man.

He continues by outlining the order of their creation. Verses 8-9:

8 For the man is not of the woman; but the woman of the man. 9 Neither was the man created for the woman; but the woman for the man.

He is speaking about woman being created from the rib God removed from Adam. (See Genesis 2:22.) Verses 10-12:

10 For this cause ought the woman to have power on her head because of the angels. 11 Nevertheless neither is the man without the woman, neither the woman without the man, in the Lord.

12 For as the woman is of the man, even so is the man also by the woman; but all things of God.

He concludes this thought by pointing out that the first woman was created from a man's rib, so are all men born from women. However, all things are from God.

I believe Paul is presenting an order that can be used to settle disputes within the assembly. To maintain this hierarchy, it must be visible in the daily affairs of the assembly. Verses 13-14:

> 13 **Judge in yourselves: is it comely [fitting or suitable] that a woman pray unto God uncovered? 14 Doth not even nature itself teach you, that, if a man have long hair, it is a shame unto him? 15 But if a woman have long hair, it is a glory to her: for her hair is given her for a covering.**

Within any group, there will be arguments, disagreements, and quarrels. Rather than chaos occurring, Paul lists above the order or structure of the assembly. Verse 16:

> 16 **But if any man seem to be contentious [quarrelsome], we have no such custom, neither the churches of God.**

Paul has heard there are divisions within the assembly and sets out some rules for order. Verses 17-18:

> 17 Now in this that I declare unto you I praise you not, that ye come together not for the better, but for the worse.

> 18 For first of all, when ye come together in the church, I hear that there be divisions among you; and I partly believe it.

First and foremost, there must be no heresies within the assembly. A heresy is a deviation from the established doctrines taught to them by the Apostle Paul. Verse 19:

> 19 For there must be also heresies among you, that they which are approved may be made manifest [evident] among you.

Those who are approved among the assembly will be *made manifest* or *made known* because of their commitment to *correct doctrine* or teaching that is *orthodox*. He continues by addressing issues concerning the Lord's supper. Many were treating it as a Jewish feast of festival and not respecting its meaningful significance. Verses 20-22:

> 20 When ye come together therefore into

one place, this is not to eat the Lord's supper.

21 For in eating every one taketh [eats] before other [another has] his own supper: and one is hungry, and another is drunken.

22 What? have ye not houses to eat and to drink in? or despise ye the church of God, and shame them that have not? What shall I say to you? shall I praise you in this? I praise you not.

Paul is not pleased with the shameful manner in their observance of the Lord's supper.

For that reason, he writes the following. This has become the manner in which most assemblies observe the Lord's supper today. Verses 23-25:

23 For I have received of the Lord that which also I delivered unto you, That the Lord Jesus the same night in which he was betrayed took bread:

24 And when he had given thanks, he brake it, and said, Take, eat: this is my body, which is broken for you: this do

in remembrance of me.

25 After the same manner also he took the cup, when he had supped, saying, This cup is the new testament in my blood: this do ye, as oft as ye drink it, in remembrance of me.

Many of you will recognize these as the words are spoken in many evangelical churches in remembrance of Christ's death. Verse 26:

26 For as often as ye eat this bread, and drink this cup, ye do shew the Lord's death till he come.

Paul wants those who partake in communion to be in a proper state of mind. Verses 27-30:

27 Wherefore whosoever shall eat this bread, and drink this cup of the Lord, unworthily, shall be guilty of the body and blood of the Lord.

28 But let a man examine himself, and so let him eat of that bread, and drink of that cup. 29 For he that eateth and drinketh unworthily, eateth and drinketh damnation to himself, not discerning the Lord's

body. 30 For this cause many are weak and sickly among you, and many sleep.

To observe communion unworthily or with lack of respect does not cause one to lose their salvation. Salvation is purchased by the blood of Christ and can never be taken away. However, actions can have an effect upon the person. Verses 31-32:

> **31 For if we would judge ourselves, we should not be judged.**
>
> **32 But when we are judged, we are chastened of [by] the Lord, that we should not be condemned [judged] with the world.**

Again, the judgment here has nothing to do with salvation. It has to do with the health and well-being of the believer and their personal testimony to the world.

He asserts that communion is not a meal to satisfy the flesh. If someone is hungry, then they should eat before partaking in communion. Verses 33-34:

> **33 Wherefore, my brethren, when ye come together to eat, tarry [wait] one for another.**

34 And if any man hunger, let him eat at home; that ye come not together unto condemnation. And the rest will I set in order when I come.

Communion is not physical. It is spiritual. It is the intimate fellowship between believers and God Who saved them.

13

1 Corinthians 12

In this chapter, Paul instructs the Corinthians on spiritual gifts. Gifts are something given without expectation of repayment. They cannot be earned. Gifts are freely given to those who receive them. We will see that these gifts are given with a purpose. They are not given to benefit the individual, but to benefit the Body of Christ as a whole. 1 Corinthians 12:1-2:

> 1 **Now concerning spiritual gifts, brethren, I would not have you ignorant. 2 Ye know that ye were Gentiles, carried away unto these dumb idols, even as ye were led.**

Gentiles, who are the non-Jews, were led astray by following after idols. These idols are *dumb* meaning they are *mute* or *unable to speak*. He provides them with a test by which they can test or try the spirits of men. Verse 3:

> 3 **Wherefore I give you to understand, that no man speaking by the Spirit of God calleth Jesus accursed: and that no man can say that Jesus is the Lord, but by the Holy Ghost.**

Paul instructs them concerning the various gifts that are given. These are talents or abilities. Notice these gifts which are given come from the *same Lord*, the *same God*, and the *same Spirit*. Verses 4-7:

> 4 **Now there are diversities of gifts, but the same Spirit.** 5 **And there are differences of administrations, but the same Lord.**
>
> 6 **And there are diversities of operations, but it is the same God which worketh all in all.**
>
> 7 **But the manifestation of the Spirit is given to every man to profit withal.**

Every believer receives the Holy Spirit and it is *manifest* or *made known* in each of them. He continues

116

by listing nine different gifts. Verses 8-11:

> **8 For to one is given by the Spirit <u>the word of wisdom</u>; to another <u>the word of knowledge</u> by the same Spirit; 9 To another <u>faith</u> by the same Spirit; to another <u>the gifts of healing</u> by the same Spirit; 10 To another <u>the working of miracles</u>; to another <u>prophecy</u>; to another <u>discerning of spirits</u>; to another <u>divers kinds of tongues</u>; to another <u>the interpretation of tongues</u>:**

> **11 But all these worketh that one and the selfsame Spirit, dividing to every man severally as he will.**

The word *severally* means *separately, distinctly, individually or apart from others.* Therefore, each gift is given to a believer separately as the Spirit chooses.

Paul begins by explaining that every believer is part of the Body of Christ. Let us look at another list of gifts and their purpose. In this way we can compare them to his list in 1 Corinthians. He writes in Ephesians 4:11-13:

> **11 And he gave some, <u>apostles</u>; and some, <u>prophets</u>; and some, <u>evangelists</u>;**

and some, <u>pastors</u> and <u>teachers</u>;

12 <u>For</u> [1] <u>the perfecting of the saints</u>, for [2] <u>the work of the ministry</u>, for [3] <u>the edifying of the body of Christ</u>:

13 Till we all come in the unity of the faith, and of the knowledge of the Son of God, unto a perfect man, unto the measure of the stature of the fulness of Christ:

The purpose of the gifts is to benefit not the recipient of the gift(s), but *all believers* who are *the Body of Christ*. Now, with this information, let us return to the text. Paul compares the body of believers with parts of a human body. 1 Corinthians 12:12-14:

12 For as the body is one, and hath many members, and all the members of that one body, being many, are one body: so also is Christ.

13 For by one Spirit are we all baptized into one body, whether we be Jews or Gentiles, whether we be bond or free; and have been all made to drink into one Spirit.

14 For the body is not one member, but many.

We see the Body of Christ is comprised of many parts, but it still functions as one body. Spiritual gifts all come from one Spirit. Verses 15-18:

15 If the foot shall say, Because I am not the hand, I am not of the body; is it therefore not of the body? 16 And if the ear shall say, Because I am not the eye, I am not of the body; is it therefore not of the body?

17 If the whole body were an eye, where were [would] the hearing [be]? If the whole [body] were hearing, where were [would] the smelling [be]?

18 But now hath God set the members every one of them in the body, as it hath pleased him.

The Spirit determines the gifts and the part each member will play in the overall body of believers. Every member benefits this singular Body of Christ.

He continues with his example. Verses 19-22:

19 **And if they were all one member, where were the body? 20 But now are they many members, yet but one body.**

21 **And the eye cannot say unto the hand, I have no need of thee: nor again the head to the feet, I have no need of you.**

22 **Nay, much more those members of the body, which seem to be more feeble, are necessary:**

No individual part of the body is more important than another. Each has its respective role in the operation of the whole. Verses 23-24:

23 **And those members of the body, which we think to be less honourable, upon these we bestow more abundant honour; and our uncomely parts have more abundant comeliness.**

24 **For our comely parts have no need: <u>but God hath tempered the body together,</u> having given more abundant honour to that part which lacked:**

You may remember the word *comely* means *that which is becoming, fit, or suitable in form or manner* while uncomely means the opposite. The key to understanding these verses is the word *tempered*. This word means *to be duly mixed or modified, reduced to a proper state, to be softened or hardened as necessary*. In other words, it is the Spirit Who *balances* every part. Why does the Spirit do this?

There is a reason. The Spirit works all things together to bring the Body of Christ into a harmonious unity so that there are no divisions. Verses 25-27:

> 25 **That there should be no schism in the body; but that the members should have the same care one for another.**
>
> 26 **And whether one member suffer, all the members suffer with it; or one member be honoured, all the members rejoice with it.**
>
> 27 **Now ye [you all] are the body of Christ, and members in particular.**

Paul tells the Corinthians what he saw him tell the Ephesians above. Now, he puts them into an order of importance. Verse 28:

> 28 **And God hath set some in the church, first apostles, secondarily prophets,**

thirdly teachers, after that miracles, then gifts of healings, helps, governments, diversities of tongues.

Each gift, talent, or ability is different. Each gift is useful to the assembly and, for that reason, not everyone receives the same gift. Verses 29-31:

29 Are all apostles? are all prophets? are all teachers? are all workers of miracles? 30 Have all the gifts of healing? do all speak with tongues? do all interpret?

31 But covet [desire] earnestly the best gifts: and yet shew I unto you a more excellent way.

In the next chapter, Paul shows us the most excellent gift to be desired.

14

1 Corinthians 13

We can say there are a lot of problems in the Corinthian assembly. Many believers are carnally minded and focus on themselves. Paul had taught them the doctrine of salvation, but many were looking to advance their own standing or position in the church. This applies to the gifts of the Spirit as well. He continues his discussion on the members of the Body of Christ and now reveals *a more excellent way*. 1 Corinthians 13:1-3:

> 1 **Though I speak with the tongues of men and of angels, and have not charity [love], I am become as sounding brass, or a tinkling cymbal.**
>
> 2 **And though I have the gift of proph-**

ecy, and understand all mysteries, and all knowledge; and though I have all faith, so that I could remove mountains, and have not charity [love], I am nothing.

3 And though I bestow all my goods to feed the poor, and though I give my body to be burned, and have not charity [love], it profiteth me nothing.

The more excellent way has to do with *love*. This is His *greatest gift*. His love is unique. It is His love He bestowed upon all of us. Remember that it was God Who commended or showed His love toward us, in that while we were yet sinners, Christ died for us. (*cf.* Rom. 5:8.) God's love never changes!

He speaks of this unique *love*, called *charity*, that God Himself demonstrates. It is important to see this. So, I included it in brackets in the following. Verses 4-7:

4 Charity [Love] suffereth long, and is kind; charity [love] envieth not; charity [love] vaunteth not itself, is not puffed up, 5 Doth not behave itself unseemly, seeketh not her own, is not easily provoked, thinketh no evil;

6 Rejoiceth not in iniquity, but rejoiceth in the truth; 7 Beareth all things, believeth all things, hopeth all things, endureth all things.

He compares *the gift of love,* called *charity,* with the lesser gifts which will diminish. Verses 8-10:

8 Charity [Love] never faileth: but whether there be prophecies, they shall fail [cease]; whether there be tongues, they shall cease; whether there be knowledge, it shall vanish away.

9 For [now] we know in part, and we prophesy in part. 10 <u>But when that which is perfect is come, then that which is in part shall be done away</u>.

This last verse is important and we need to discuss this. Paul makes a reference to a point in time because he uses the word *when.* He says *when that which is perfect is come,* these gifts will cease. There are a couple of interpretations of this last verse.

Remember, Paul is addressing grace believers and his message is for the Age of Grace. Why? It is because they are gone after the Rapture. So, he cannot be speaking about the Second Coming as that occurs at the end of the Tribulation and grace believers are removed seven years prior to His Coming. Therefore, *when that which is perfect is come* can only refer to *His Coming for His saints.* Thereafter, grace believers, called saints, will be in the presence of the Lord forever. The gifts were given temporarily to edify the body of believers who wait for the Rapture, arriving in heaven will make the gifts redundant. The gifts would no longer serve their purpose and cease.

There is another interpretation. It has to do with the words *when that which is perfect is come.* There is only One Who is *perfect* and He is the Lord Jesus Christ. Jesus Christ is the *Word of God.* (See John 1:1.) Therefore, *that which is perfect is come* could refer to the completed Bible – the authoritative *Word of God.* Many believe when the written Word of God was completed, the gifts ceased. This is a point of contention especially with charismatic believers who refer to this as the *cessation of gifts.* Paul told us that the purpose of the gifts is to edify the body. Many believe the gifts no longer operate because "… we walk by faith, not by sight" (2 Cor. 5:7). Since the Word of God is the authority established by God, we are limited to its revelation. Nothing can be added or taken away from it. (See Rev. 22:18-19.) Regardless of the interpretation we choose to use, we must know this:

nothing can be added to or taken away from the completed, inspired, and infallible Word of God for what we have in God's Word is perfect!

I will leave you with this thought. As believers, we can be sure that the Holy Spirit resides in us. He is our earnest or guaranty of the completed redemption of the purchased possession. (See Eph. 1:13-14.) This same Holy Spirit Who inspired the writers of the Scripture also illuminates the Scriptures for all who look for its meaning. As a writer and teacher of God's Word, I give all the credit and glory to the Holy Spirit if I have accomplished anything of value. Many people forget with Whom they are dealing when they read the Bible. If you need help, it would please the Holy Spirit if you asked Him for His help and waited for His reply.

What we are studying now in Corinthians is undoubtedly *meat* for mature believers. As each of us continue to grow in doctrine and faith we must put away things we learned as a child. Verse 11:

> 11 **When I was a child, I spake as a child, I understood as a child, I thought as a child: but when I became a man, I put away childish things.**

Today, we can only see in part. Someday, when we

see Christ face to face, we will know Christ in the same manner as He knows us. Verse 12:

> 12 **For now we see through a glass, darkly; but then [later] face to face: now I know in part; but then [later] shall I know even as also I am known.**

Paul wants all grace believers to focus on *a more excellent way*. Verse 13:

> 13 **And now abideth faith, hope, charity, [love] these three; but the greatest of these is charity [love].**

The gifts of the Spirit are not meant to elevate some above others. They are to edify the Body of Christ. Gifts are tools. They are given to be used by believers in their ministry. Who are those who do the ministry? Paul told us that God gave some to be apostles; and some to be prophets; and some to be evangelists; and some to be pastors and teachers. Why? It is for the perfecting of the saints, for the work of the ministry, and for *the edifying of the body of Christ!* (See Eph. 4:11-12.)

15

1 Corinthians 14

Paul continues with his teaching on *the gifts of the Spirit.* 1 Corinthians 14:1:

> 1 **Follow after charity, and desire spiritual gifts, but rather that ye may prophesy.**

Believers are to first seek the gift of love because it is the greatest gift. This is followed by the gift of prophecy. Here, *prophesy* is not referring to predicting the future. Instead, it means *to speak the Word of God or to preach it.* I like to think of *prophecy* today as proclaiming the *Word of God.* This would be instructing in doctrine, and interpreting or explaining Scripture. It also includes exhorting others to apply its teaching. Compare this to what Paul wrote in Ephesians 4:11-12:

11 And he gave some, [to be] apostles; and some, [to be] prophets; and some, [to be] evangelists; and some, [to be] pastors and teachers;

12 <u>For the perfecting of the saints, for the work of the ministry, for the edifying of the body of Christ:</u>

Note that these gifts are given to benefit the believers — *the perfecting of the saints.* Individuals are not to personally profit from the gifts they receive. They are *for the edifying of the body of Christ.*

The gift of tongues is often misunderstood. It might help us to understand it from seeing it in the light of the purpose of the gifts. In Corinth, it was causing division and contention within the assembly. Due to these issue, Paul will deal with the gift of tongues for the remainder of this chapter. 1 Corinthians 14:2-5:

2 For he that speaketh in an unknown tongue speaketh not unto men, but unto God: for no man understandeth him; howbeit in the spirit he speaketh mysteries.

3 But he that prophesieth [preacheth]

speaketh unto men to edification, and exhortation, and comfort. 4 He that speaketh in an unknown tongue edifieth himself; but he that prophesieth [preacheth] edifieth the church.

5 I would that ye all spake with tongues, but rather [instead] that ye prophesied: for greater is he that prophesieth [preacheth] than he that speaketh with tongues, except he interpret, that the church may receive edifying.

Let us stop for a moment to consider this. We will start by repeating what we already know. The purpose of the spiritual gifts is to *edify the Body of Christ*. Next, in this context, *prophesy* does not mean fortune-telling. It does not mean predicting the future. It means *to preach, to instruct in doctrine, to interpret or explain Scripture, and to exhort others to apply its teaching*. In the same way that preaching is to edify the believers, so too is prophecy and the gift of tongues to edify the Body of Christ.

When it comes to the use of the gift of tongues, there must be someone present to interpret it. Otherwise, there is no edification of the Body of Christ and the purpose of the gift is not served. Verses: 6-10:

6 Now, brethren, if I come unto you speaking with tongues, what shall I profit you, except I shall speak to you either by revelation, or by knowledge, or by prophesying, or by doctrine?

7 And even things without life giving sound, whether pipe or harp, except they give a distinction in the sounds, how shall it be known what is piped or harped? 8 For if the trumpet give an uncertain sound, who shall prepare himself to the battle?

9 So likewise ye [you all], except ye [you all] utter by the tongue words easy to be understood, how shall it be known what is spoken? for ye [you all] shall speak into the air.

10 There are, it may be, so many kinds of voices in the world, and none of them is without signification [distinction].

Each voice or language must be recognized to be understood. Of all the languages in the world, none of them is without *signification. Signification* is *the act of making known, or of communicating ideas to another by signs or by words, by anything that is understood, partic-*

ularly by words. This would even include *signing* for the deaf because their signing has meaning.

From this, Paul draws the following conclusion. Verse 11:

> 11 Therefore <u>if I know not the meaning of the voice</u>, [then] <u>I shall be unto him that speaketh a barbarian,</u> <u>and he that speaketh shall be a barbarian unto me</u>.

In this context, the word *barbarian* has a particular meaning. Greeks and Romans considered most foreign nations to be *barbarians* because many were ignorant of their language, laws, and customs. Most importantly, neither could be understood.

The Corinthians were eager to get ahead, advance in the assembly and to differentiate themselves. This *zeal* was unfortunately from *an eagerness or desire to accomplish or obtain something for themselves*. For this reason, they eagerly sought to obtain spiritual gifts. Verse 12:

> 12 Even so ye, forasmuch as ye are zealous of spiritual gifts, [rather] seek that ye may excel to the edifying of the church.

Instead, they should seek to edify or build up the believers and, in seeking this, they will receive what the Spirit deems necessary according to their need. Again, we see the purpose of the gifts is to edify!

Paul addresses those who speak in unknown tongues using himself as an example. Verses 13-14:

> 13 **Wherefore let him that speaketh in an unknown tongue pray that he may interpret. 14 For if I pray in an unknown tongue, my spirit prayeth, but my understanding is unfruitful.**

There is no benefit to speaking in tongues unless the words can be understood. If they cannot, then they are unfruitful or of no advantage to the hearer. He tells believers to pray and ask God for someone to interpret the words. In this way, all believers will benefit. Verses 15-17:

> 15 **What is it then? I will pray with the spirit, and I will pray with the understanding also: I will sing with the spirit, and I will sing with the understanding also.**

> 16 **Else when thou shalt bless with the spirit, how shall he that occupieth the**

room of the unlearned say Amen at thy giving of thanks, seeing he understandeth not what thou sayest?

17 For thou verily [truly] givest thanks well, but the other [not understanding] is not edified.

Paul states that he often speaks in tongues and praises God privately. Publicly, the spiritual gifts are to edify the Body of Christ. He makes a comparison between speaking a few words that are understood and speaking many in an unknown tongue. Verses 18-19:

18 I thank my God, [that] I speak with tongues more than ye all: 19 Yet in the church I had [would] rather speak five words with my understanding, that by my voice I might teach others also, than ten thousand words in an unknown tongue.

Again, I think we are beginning to see the gifts from Paul's perspective. The purpose of the spiritual gifts is to edify the Body of Christ. The opposite of understanding is ignorance. Verse 20:

20 Brethren, be not children in under-

standing: howbeit [how can it be that] in malice be ye children, but in understanding be men.

Paul choose the word *malice* which is a powerful word. It means *extreme hatred* or *an intent to injure others out of spite*. How is it possible for believers to act in malice as immature children and also understand his teaching like mature adults?

He quotes the prophet Isaiah who was speaking to the rebellious Jews. They are not listening to Isaiah speak about the "times of refreshing" when the kingdom will be established. So, God sent them another messenger, the Assyrians! They would speak a foreign language from other lips and they still would not hear God. (*cf.* Isa. 28:9-13.) Verse 21:

21 In the law it is written, With men of other tongues and other lips will I speak unto this people; and yet for all that will they not hear me, saith the Lord.

Like Israel, there are those who seek revelation outside His Word. Israel has Isaiah. The Body of Christ has the Word of God. Still, some seek a message from tongues which is impossible to understand without a correct interpretation. Yet, they have the perfect

Word of God. The Bible is sufficient.

Paul explains that the gift of tongues is a more effective sign for unbelievers. Verse 22:

> 22 Wherefore tongues are for a sign, not to them that believe, but to them that believe not: but prophesying [preaching] serveth not for them that believe not, but for them which believe.

Prophesy, or preaching, serves those who believe. But, for those who do not believe. "… faith cometh by hearing, and hearing by the word of God" (Rom. 10:17). Verses 23-24:

> 23 If therefore the whole church be come together into one place, and all speak with tongues, and there come in those that are unlearned, or unbelievers, will they not say that ye are mad?

> 24 But if all prophesy [preaching], and there come in one that believeth not, or one unlearned, he is convinced of [by] all, he is judged of all:

An unbeliever comes in and hears the Word of God preached. He listens to all that is presented. Confronted by his deep thoughts, he is convicted by the truth. Verse 25:

> 25 And thus are the secrets of his heart made manifest; and so falling down on his face he will worship God, and report that God is in you of a truth.

When believers gather together, Paul wants all things to edify both the believers and those who do not believe but come to hear. Verse 26:

> 26 How is it then, brethren? when ye come together, every one of you hath a psalm, hath a doctrine, hath a tongue, hath a revelation, hath an interpretation. Let all things be done unto edifying.

To assure order is maintained within the assembly, he instructs them as follows. Verses 27-33:

> 27 If any man speak in an unknown tongue, let it be by two, or at the most by three, and that by course; and let one interpret. 28 But if there be no interpreter, let him keep silence in the church; and let him speak to himself, and to God.

29 Let the prophets speak two or three, and let the other judge. **30** If any thing be revealed to another that sitteth by, let the first hold his peace. **31** For ye may all prophesy [preach] one by one [one at a time], that all may learn, and all may be comforted.

32 And the spirits of the prophets are subject to the prophets. **33** For God is not the author of confusion, but of peace, as in all churches [assemblies] of the saints.

It is necessary to interject something here. The letters to Corinth were written at the beginning of Paul's ministry. There were no other letters to which the believers could refer. Except for the teachings of Paul, it was limited to others who would speak under the influence of the Holy Spirit. During this time, Paul instructs that other preachers, or prophets, in attendance should confirm the words being spoken. Once the Bible was completed, it became the sole authority to which every believer could turn for the truth.

He seeks to establish order within the assemblies. Verses 34-35:

34 Let your women keep silence in the churches [assemblies]: for it is not permitted unto them to speak; but they are commanded to be under obedience, as also saith the law.

35 And if they will [desire to] learn any thing, let them ask their husbands at home: for it is a shame for women to speak in the church [assembly].

He asks two questions. Was it you who brought the Word of God? Did the Word of God come only to you? Verse 36:

36 What? came the word of God out from you? or came it unto you only?

Any man who wants to preach and teach the Word of God must first acknowledge that the words which Paul teaches or writes to them are the commandments of God. Verse 37:

37 If any man think himself to be a prophet, or spiritual, let him acknowledge that the things that I write unto you are the commandments of the Lord.

Paul was appointed to be *the* Apostle to the Gentles by the Risen Lord. (*cf.* Gal. 1:1.)

There are those who understand Paul's teachings and those who are ignorant. Here, the word *ignorant* means *uninstructed, uninformed, or untaught*. It does not mean stupid. Verse 38:

> 38 **But if any man be ignorant, let him be ignorant.**

Those who are *untaught* in the assembly should be known by the believers and, therefore, ignored. Let those who understand and are able to teach instruct them so that they will no longer be *ignorant*. This make the gift of prophecy—the ability to teach and instruct—of great value. Verse 39:

> 39 **Wherefore, brethren, covet [desire] to prophesy [teach], and forbid not to speak with tongues.**

I think Paul has made his point. The purpose of the spiritual gifts is to edify and build up the Body of Christ. Everything that is done in the assembly must be done *decently*, meaning *upright and respectable*, and *in order*. This will glorify God. Verse 40:

40 Let all things be done decently and in order.

16

1 Corinthians 15 (Part I)

Paul is concerned that the gospel which he was given by the Risen Lord remain unchanged. I sometimes test an average Christian by asking, "Can you tell me how I can be saved? How can you be confident that you are eternally saved and going to heaven?" From their answer to this question, I will know their understanding of the gospel. Here is the most concise statement of Paul's gospel. It is found in 1 Corinthians 15:1-4:

> 1 Moreover, brethren, I declare unto you the gospel which I preached unto you, which also ye have received, and wherein ye stand; 2 By which also ye are saved, if ye keep in memory what I preached unto you, unless ye have believed in vain.

3 For <u>I delivered unto you first of all that which I also received,</u> how that [1] Christ died for our sins according to the scriptures; 4 And that [2] he was buried, and that [3] he rose again the third day according to the scriptures:

First, note his statement says *the gospel.* It does not use the indefinite article saying *a gospel,* but the definite article saying *the gospel.* Paul is making it clear to the Corinthians that this is *the only gospel by which ye are saved.*

Someday, if you have an opportunity to look in a church hymnal, look up this hymn written by J. Wilbur Chapman. It is entitled *One Day.* I mention this because the refrain of this hymn summaries Paul's Gospel of Grace.

> Living, He loved me;
> Dying, He saved me;
> Buried, He carried my sins far away;
> Rising, He justified freely forever:
> One day He's coming — O glorious day!

How simple is Paul's gospel: Christ did it all! How can we possibly add anything to the word which He has already finished? The answer is, "We cannot." His completed work is sufficient to save us. Any-

144

thing we add to what God has already completed will only diminish its sufficiency!

Paul spends the majority of his ministry presenting the Gospel of the Grace of God. The remainder of his time he spends defending it from being altered. Here, in his letter to the believers in Galatia, he deals with this very issue. Galatians 1:6-8:

> 6 I marvel <u>that ye are so soon removed</u> from him [me] that [who] called you into the grace of Christ <u>unto another gospel</u>:
>
> 7 <u>Which is not another [gospel]</u>; but there be some that trouble you, and would pervert the gospel of Christ. 8 But though we, or an angel from heaven, preach any other gospel unto you than that which we have preached unto you, let him be accursed.

This is so important that Paul repeats himself in verse 9:

> 9 As we said before, so say I now again, <u>If any man preach any other gospel unto you than that ye have received, let him be accursed.</u>

We might stop and think about the simplicity of this gospel message. Why do many present-day churches not preach this simple message? Instead, they altered it. Works, obligations, and requirements are added by man. This has been the case from the very beginning. In his last letter before his death, here are the words he writes. 2 Timothy 1:15:

> **15 [Timothy,] This thou knowest, that all they which are in Asia be turned away from me . . .**

He is speaking about the seven churches he established in Asia Minor (the area now Turkey). Before his death, all of them had departed from his teaching. Seminaries train pastors and those pastors teach the people the progressive "history of the church." They do not realize that the church had departed from the truth of Paul's simple gospel. How much more have they added to what was already sufficient. Paul warns of this in Colossians 2:8:

> **8 Beware lest any man spoil you <u>through philosophy and vain deceit, after the tradition of men, after the rudiments of the world, and not after Christ.</u>**

He continues with 1 Corinthians 15:5-8:

5 And that he [Christ] was seen of Cephas, then of the twelve: 6 After that, he was seen of above five hundred brethren at once; of whom the greater part remain [alive] unto this present [day], but some are fallen asleep.

7 After that, he was seen of James; then of all the apostles. 8 <u>And last of all he was seen of me [Paul] also, as of one born out of due time.</u>

He ends with a statement concerning his own salvation. This occurred *after* Christ's death, burial, and resurrection. His meeting with the Risen Savior was *out of due time* since Paul's time was after Christ's earthly ministry with the Twelve. What was the reason for this?

Paul's meeting was delayed because it was according to the will of God. He explains this in Romans 15:8:

8 Now I say that Jesus Christ was a minister of the circumcision [the Jews] for the truth of God, [why?] to confirm the promises made unto the fathers:

Christ and the Twelve preached *the Gospel of the*

Kingdom. However, Paul carried a different gospel. He carries *the Gospel of the Grace of God.* Paul explains this to the Gentiles in Romans 11:25-27:

> 25 **For I would [desire] not, brethren, that ye should be ignorant of this mystery, lest ye should be wise in your own conceits; <u>that blindness in part is happened to Israel, until the fulness of the Gentiles be come in.</u>**
>
> 26 **And so all [true] Israel shall be saved: as it is written, There shall come out of Sion the Deliverer, and shall turn away ungodliness from Jacob: 27 For this is my covenant unto them [Israel], when I shall take away their sins.**

This is critical for our understanding. We must see that the Apostle Paul was separate from the other apostles. 1 Corinthians 15:9-11:

> 9 **For I am the least of the apostles, that am not meet [suitable] to be called an apostle, because I persecuted the church of God.**
>
> 10 **But by the grace of God I am what I am: and his grace which was bestowed**

upon me was not in vain; but I laboured more abundantly than they all: yet not I, but the grace of God which was with me.

11 **Therefore whether it were I or they, so we preach, and so ye believed.**

Paul once persecuted those who followed Christ and the Kingdom Gospel. We are first introduced to him at the stoning of Stephen. You can read the entire story in Acts chapters 6 and 7. The story ends with this, "And Saul [Paul] was consenting unto his [Stephen's] death . . ." (Acts 8:1). Is it not interesting that, at such a point in the Bible, we are first introduced to Paul who had never been mentioned before?

Paul continues by refuting another false doctrine. There are those who say there is no resurrection. Verses 12-15:

12 **Now if Christ be preached that he rose from the dead, how say some among you that there is no resurrection of the dead? 13 But if there be no resurrection of the dead, then is Christ not risen:**

14 **And if Christ be not risen, then is our**

preaching vain, and your faith is also vain. 15 Yea, and we are found false witnesses of God; because we have testified of God that he raised up Christ: whom he raised not up, if so be that the dead rise not.

How critical is the resurrection to *the gospel?* It is the very foundation of salvation! Can you see that his gospel was continually under attack by Satan and the children of darkness?

Paul argues that without the resurrection, all is vanity or emptiness. There is no hope! Verses 16-19:

16 For if the dead rise not, then is not Christ raised: 17 And <u>if Christ be not raised, your faith is vain;</u> ye are yet in your sins.

18 Then they also which are fallen asleep in Christ are perished. 19 If in this life only we have hope in Christ, we are of all men most miserable.

Thank God that the above is not the case. Resurrection does exist and Christ is the proof of it. Verse 20:

20 But now is Christ risen from the dead,

**and [He has] become the firstfruits of
them that slept.**

Christ is often referred to as the *only begotten* because
He was the first to be raised from the dead. (*cf.* Ps.
2:7.) Because of this, others can also be raised who
believe and have faith in His death, burial, and resurrection.

To understand the sufficiency of the role Christ
paid in the effectiveness of salvation, Paul compares
Christ to Adam. Friend, the next two verses are theological meat. If one swallows meat without chewing
it first, then they get theological indigestion. Think
about this. In the following, notice that each man was
the first and, therefore, a representative of the whole.
Verse 21:

**21 For since by man [Adam] came death,
by man [Jesus] came also the resurrection of the dead.**

Adam's sinning resulted in condemnation for all.
However, through Christ, all—that means everyone—will be resurrected from the dead. Some will be
resurrected to eternal life; others to eternal damnation. Verse 22:

22 For as [it is] <u>in Adam all die</u>, even so

in Christ shall all be made alive.

This last verse is important enough to repeat. If the word *all* means *everyone,* then it is telling us that *all people* will be resurrected from the dead. Do not confuse this with *universal salvation* which teaches that everyone will be *saved.* That is far from the truth! Jesus spoke to the Jews with His words recorded in John 5:28-29:

> 28 **Marvel not at this: for the hour is coming, in the which <u>all that are in the graves</u> shall hear his voice,**
>
> 29 **And <u>shall come forth; they that have done good, unto the resurrection of life</u>; and <u>they that have done evil, unto the resurrection of damnation.</u>**

God Who created *the heaven and the earth* also raised Christ from the dead. This same power will raise *all* the dead from their graves! One man was the cause of death while Another obtained victory over death. Paul writes in Romans 5:17:

> 17 **For if <u>by one man's offence [Adam] death reigned</u> by one; much more <u>they which receive abundance of grace and of the gift of righteousness shall reign</u>**

152

in [everlasting] life by one, Jesus Christ.

Here is a good point for us to take a break. We will finish 1 Corinthians 15 in the next chapter. In the meantime consider the power of God. The same power He used for creation is the same power He uses for resurrection from the dead.

17

1 Corinthians 15 (Part II)

As Adam's fall brought God's judgment and condemnation upon both Man and Creation, His Son provided the singular solution. Through Christ's righteous life and sacrificial death, the penalty for sin was paid in full. God showed His love for the world by giving only His Son. John 3:16-17:

> 16 **For God so loved the world, that he gave his only begotten Son, that whosoever believeth in him should not perish, but have everlasting life.**

> 17 **For God sent not his Son into the world to condemn the world; but that the world through him might be saved.**

This single act provides the solution for both Jew and Gentile. Jews can be saved by the Gospel of the Kingdom. Gentiles can be saved by the Gospel of Grace. Each is made possible by the finished work of Jesus Christ. His selfless act is the justification for resurrection of the dead – for everyone! This is not universal salvation as we must see how this justification is applied.

In the previous chapter, we learned that all mankind will be resurrected. Shortly, we will see that some will be resurrected to eternal life while others to eternal judgment. All those who believe that after death there are no consequences will be sadly mistaken. When will this resurrection take place? Paul gives us an order in which this will happen. It began with the resurrection of Jesus Christ. It is for that reason He is called "the first begotten by the Father" because He is the first to be raised from the dead. With that said, we can return to 1 Corinthians 15:23:

> **23 But every man in his own order: [first] Christ the firstfruits; [then] afterward they that are Christ's at his coming.**

There are two distinct future events. We must not get them confused. There is *Christ's Coming* for the Body of Christ which is called the "Appearing." (See 1 Thess. 4:16-18.) This will be the bodily redemption of grace believers and will complete their redemption. (See Eph. 1:13-14.) Then, there is *His Second Coming* which is His return to earth in His role as the King. This will occur at the end of the Tribulation.

Paul speaks of this final victory in the next verse. Grace believers will be removed when He "appears" and calls them to Himself. Those who remain will be Jews and unsaved Gentiles. Paul speaks about the time following the Tribulation. Verse 24:

> 24 **Then cometh the end, when he [Christ] shall have delivered up the kingdom to God, even [that is to say] the Father; when he shall have put down [subdued] all rule and all authority and power.**

For the Jews, it has always been about the Kingdom of David and their Messiah reigning as the eternal King. This is dealt with in depth in the book *The Glorious Destiny of Israel–The Fulfillment of God's Promises and Prophecies to Israel.* It has a long title, but it is a great book and will answer questions about Israel and their future.

God the Father must continue to reign until all His enemies have been subdued. Once Creation has been restored to its purity, then Christ shall reign. Verses 25-27:

> 25 For he [God] must reign, till he hath put all enemies under his feet. 26 The last enemy that shall be destroyed is death.

> 27 For he hath put all things under his feet. But when he saith all things are put under him, it is manifest that he [Christ] is excepted, which [Who] did put all things under him [God].

All things will be put under God's feet with one exception. This exception is the One Who put all things under God's feet—His only Son, Jesus Christ. Christ will have accomplished all this for His Father. Notice what Christ does. Verse 28:

> 28 And when all things shall be subdued unto him [God], then shall the Son also [make] himself be subject unto him [God] that [Christ Who] put all things under him [God], [so] that God may be all in all.

When all is subdued except Christ Who is the Victor, what does He do? He willingly subjects Himself to the Father. For what reason does He do this? He does this so *that God may be all in all!*

Paul continues with the hypothetical question, "What if there is not resurrection from the dead?" There are some religions who have living relatives baptized on behalf of those who have already died. Verse 29:

> 29 **Else what shall they do which are baptized for the dead, if the dead rise not at all? why are they then baptized for the dead?**

Whether being baptized for themselves or someone else, if there is no resurrection from the dead, then why would anyone do it? In the following, the word *jeopardy* means *being exposed to death.* Verse 30:

> 30 **And why stand we in jeopardy every hour?**

Paul's letters are intended to be read aloud in the assemblies. His point is that without the resurrection, there is no hope. There is nothing. Paul dies daily to self, however, he has hope! In the following, the word *protest* means *to affirm with solemnity; to make a solemn declaration of a fact or opinion.* Verse 31:

> 31 **I protest [affirm] by your rejoicing which I have in Christ Jesus our Lord, I die daily.**

What benefit is it for Paul to fight the battles in order to present the Gospel of Grace? Whether he refers to fights with the spiritual realm or humans, what benefit is it to him if there is no resurrection? Verse 32:

> 32 **If after the manner of men I have fought with beasts at Ephesus, what advantageth it [to] me, if the dead rise not? let us eat and drink; for tomorrow we die.**

In response to his question, he replies as one unsaved who seeks earthly pleasures. If there is no resurrection from the dead, then *let us eat and drink; for tomorrow we die.*

Having presented a *what if* scenario, Paul continues his teaching. He tells the Corinthians not to be deceived by such foolishness. Wake up! The argument that there is no resurrection is a corruption of sound doctrine. Some within your assembly do not know God — meaning His Word. Verses 33-34:

> 33 **Be not deceived: evil communications corrupt good manners.** 34 **Awake to righteousness, and sin not; for some have not the knowledge of God: I speak this to your shame.**

Why do these people not know God? He uses the word *shame* which means *a painful sensation caused by the realization of guilt*. Why are they not teaching them in the assembly?

The Gospel of Grace is built upon the belief of Christ's death, burial and resurrection. Therefore, understanding and believing in the *resurrection* is essential. Verses 35-38:

> 35 **But some man will say, How are the dead raised up? and with what body do they come?** 36 **Thou fool, that which thou sowest [plant] is not quickened [brought to life],** <u>except it die</u>**:**

> 37 **And that which thou sowest, thou sowest not that body that shall be, but bare grain, it may chance of wheat, or of some other grain:** 38 **But God giveth it a body as it hath pleased him, and to every seed his own body.**

In his example he relates *resurrection* to seeds of grain. In whatever form, seeds are dead and must be planted or buried before they can be *quickened* or brought to life.

All living things have different flesh or type of

form. Verse 39:

> 39 **All flesh is not the same flesh: but there is one kind of flesh of men, another flesh of beasts, another of fishes, and another of birds.**

There are heavenly or celestial bodies. There are earthly or terrestrial bodies. Both have their own unique glory as each was created by God. Verse 40:

> 40 **There are also celestial bodies, and bodies terrestrial: but the glory of the celestial is one, and the glory of the terrestrial is another.**

This applies to all of God's Creation. Verse 41:

> 41 **There is one glory of the sun, and another glory of the moon, and another glory of the stars: for one star differeth from another star in glory.**

Each star is different from all the others. That is how God created them. His comparison is to teach that we too are all unique.

Paul compares the state before resurrection and afterwards. We know that only God can bring to life that which is dead. This included Adam who was once red clay until God breathed into him the breath of life. Genesis 2:7:

> 7 **And the LORD God formed man of the dust of the ground, and breathed into his nostrils the breath of life; and man became a living soul.**

Let us continue with 1 Corinthians 15:42-43:

> 42 **So also is the resurrection of the dead. It is sown in corruption; it is raised in incorruption: 43 It is sown in dishonour; it is raised in glory: it is sown in weakness; it is raised in power:**

Think about how many advertisements provide a before and after picture. This is what Paul is doing for the Corinthians. He wants them to understand the power of the resurrection. Without it, they would be lost leaving them without hope.

When we were born, we received a natural body, a body of flesh. Due to sin and our fallen nature, this body must die. Unless it die, like the seed planted, it cannot be *quickened* or *brought to life*. Verses 44-45:

44 It is sown a natural body; it is raised a spiritual body. There is a natural body, and there is a spiritual body.

45 And so it is written, The first man Adam was made a living soul; the last Adam [Christ] was made a quickening spirit.

The first Adam was created in the garden and had a natural body. Paul refers to the resurrected Lord Jesus Christ as the second Adam. When He was resurrected, He received a spiritual body. This is the same body that all those saved by grace, the Body of Christ, will receive at *His Calling* — the Rapture.

Paul continues with a comparison that confirms the above statement. Verses 46-48:

46 Howbeit that was not first which is spiritual, but that which is natural; and afterward that which is spiritual.

47 The first man [Adam] is of the earth, earthy: [while] the second man is the Lord from heaven. **48** As is the earthy, such are they also that are earthy: and as is the heavenly, such are they also that are heavenly.

Here is the most wonderful promise we could receive and it is because we are saved. This promise is sometimes called the *Blessed Hope*. It is our assurance that those who are saved by grace through faith will, like Christ, receive heavenly bodies. We who were once earthy or natural, will be like Christ Who is spiritual. Verse 49:

> **49 And as we have borne the image of the earthy, we shall also bear the image of the heavenly.**

As we await our glorious transformation, we will struggle with our earthy bodies as they age. The wonderful news is that this body, for us, is only temporary. At *His Calling*, we will be like him!

In the following, he refers to our mortal bodies as *flesh and blood*. Our transformation will be completed in an instant. He refers to this as the *twinkling of an eye*. How and when will this happen? Paul explains in verses 50-52:

> **50 Now this I say, brethren, that flesh and blood cannot inherit the kingdom of God; neither doth corruption inherit incorruption.**
>
> **51 <u>Behold, I shew you a mystery; We</u>**

> **shall not all sleep, but we shall all be changed, 52 In a moment, in the twinkling of an eye, at the last trump: for the trumpet shall sound, and the dead shall be raised incorruptible, and we shall be changed.**

When a body dies it begins to decompose. It is no longer living and sustained by the breath of life. We know our bodies are corruptible based upon sickness and the effects of aging.

The following is, in my opinion, the most powerful of Paul's doctrine on the resurrection. He teaches how this will happen. We are taken from being made corruptible to being made incorruptible. Verse 53:

> **53 For this corruptible must put on incorruption, and this mortal must put on immortality.**

What will happen when this transformation occurs? Verses 54-56:

> **54 So when this corruptible [body] shall have put on incorruption, and this mortal [body] shall have put on immortality, then shall be brought to pass the**

saying that is written, Death is swallowed up in victory.

55 O death, where is thy sting? O grave, where is thy victory? 56 The sting of death is sin; and the strength of sin is the law.

The Law does not lead to salvation. The Law leads to condemnation and judgment. For sin is the breaking of the Law and the penalty of sin is death. However, Christ fulfilled the Law completely. His fulfilling the Law gives us victory over sin and death. Through His righteousness, we are no longer subject to condemnation. Paul writes Romans 8:1-2:

1 There is therefore now no condemnation to them which are in Christ Jesus, who walk not after the flesh, but after the Spirit.

2 For the law of the Spirit of life in Christ Jesus hath made me free from the law of sin and death.

The victory belongs to Christ. His victory is the basis for our salvation. Through our faith in His finished work, we receive His righteousness and are, therefore, no longer subject to condemnation and its penalty which is death. 1 Corinthians 15:57:

> **57 But thanks be to God, which giveth us the victory through our Lord Jesus Christ.**

Many times Paul is carried away and he pauses to offer words of praise and adoration. Consider the words from the hymn written by Eugene Bartlett, Sr. entitled Victory In Jesus:

> O victory in Jesus, my Savior, forever!
> He sought me and bought me with His redeeming blood;
> He loved me ere I knew Him, and all my love is due Him.
> He plunged me to victory beneath the cleansing flood.

Believers must hold onto the promises like an anchor grips the Solid Rock. Paul tells them to hold onto solid doctrine. Be immovable. Abound in good works with gratitude. Verse 58:

> **58 Therefore, my beloved brethren, <u>be ye stedfast, unmoveable, always abounding in the work of the Lord</u>, forasmuch as ye know that your labour is not in vain in the Lord.**

18

1 Corinthians 16

At the beginning of Chapter 16, Paul makes a reference to an historical meeting that took place between the Apostle Paul and the Twelve. This meeting was briefly mentioned in the Introduction. There is a clear division between the recipients of their respective gospel messages. We can see from Galatians they agree that Peter will take his gospel to the *circumcision* which are the Jews. Paul will take his to the *uncircumcision* which is the Gentiles. You can read the entire story in the second chapter of Galatians. Towards the end of this meeting, Peter makes one request of Paul. Galatians 2:9-10:

> 9 **And when James, Cephas [Peter], and John, who seemed to be pillars, perceived the grace that was given unto me, they gave to me and Barnabas the right**

**hands of fellowship; that we should go
unto the heathen [non-Jews], and they
unto the circumcision [Jews].**

**10 Only they would [desired] that we
should remember the poor; the same
which I also was forward [willing] to
do.**

He was taking this collection throughout his missionary trips. It was a collection for the Kingdom Believers in Jerusalem. When he finally delivered the
contributions from the Grace Believers, he was ar-
rested in Jerusalem and sent to Rome for trial.

We begin with 1 Corinthians 16:1:

**1 Now concerning the collection for the
saints [in Jerusalem], as I have given order to the churches of Galatia, even so
[as I also] do ye.**

He tells the Corinthians, as he told the Galatians, that
on the first day of the week, Sunday, they should
gather funds together for his coming. Verses 2-3:

**2 Upon the first day of the week let
every one of you lay by him in store, as
God hath prospered him, that there be**

no gatherings when I come.

3 And when I come, whomsoever ye shall approve by your letters, them will I send to bring your liberality [gifts] unto Jerusalem.

If he is unable to come to collect the funds, then they should approve someone to bring the funds to him in Jerusalem. However, if it is *meet* or *acceptable*, then their emissary will go with him. Verse 4:

4 And if it be meet that I go also, they shall go with me.

It is his hope to visit them and possibly spend the winter there in Corinth. Should this happen, they can then send him on his journey. Verses 5-7:

5 Now I will come unto you, when I shall pass through Macedonia: for I do pass through Macedonia.

6 And it may be that I will abide, yea, and winter with you, that ye may bring me on my journey whithersoever I go.

7 For I will not see you now by the way; but I trust to tarry a while with you,

if the Lord permit.

He always seeks to work under the approval of the One Who appointed him. He is His Apostle and serves at the will and pleasure of the Lord Jesus Christ.

Pentecost is the very first part of harvest time in late summer. For that reason, it is a Jewish holiday called the Harvest of the First Fruits. You may recall the harvest which Jesus spoke of in the gospels. This harvest was delayed. The Jewish leaders had rejected their Messiah and the fulfillment of the Kingdom Prophecy was temporarily postponed. Verses 8-9:

> **8 But I will tarry at Ephesus until Pentecost. 9 For a great door and effectual is opened unto me, and there are many adversaries.**

Paul was planning to spend the summer in Ephesus until the early harvest, then he would make his way to those in Corinth. He planned to spend the winter with them on the southern coast of Greece overlooking the Mediterranean Sea. He calls the opportunity to share the gospel "a great door" which God has opened. He is aware of the opposition or adversaries who are determined to destroy him. However, their time has not yet come.

Paul hopes to send Timothy to Corinth to strengthen them in their faith. Timothy was taught by Paul. He considered him to be capable but lacking in boldness when dealing with the opposition. Verses 10-11:

> 10 **Now if Timotheus come, see that he may be with you without fear: for he worketh the work of the Lord, as I also do.**

> 11 **Let no man therefore despise him: but conduct him forth in peace, that he may come unto me: for I look for him with the brethren.**

Timothy was young and some of the people he would be teaching would be older and contentious.

Apollos is another teacher of grace. He is first mentioned in the book of Acts. Paul also desires to send him to the Corinthians as well. Verse 12:

> 12 **As touching our brother Apollos, I greatly desired him to come unto you with the brethren: but his will was not at all to come at this time; but he will come when he shall have convenient time.**

There is an interesting story about Apollos in Acts 18:24-27:

> 24 And <u>a certain Jew named Apollos, born at Alexandria,</u> an eloquent man, and mighty in the scriptures, came to Ephesus.

> 25 This man was instructed in the way of the Lord; and being fervent in the spirit, he spake and taught diligently the things of the Lord, knowing only the baptism of John.

> 26 And <u>he began to speak boldly in the synagogue:</u> whom <u>when Aquila and Priscilla had heard, they took him unto them, and expounded unto him the way of God more perfectly.</u>

> 27 And when he was disposed to pass into Achaia, the brethren wrote, exhorting the disciples to receive him: who, when he was come, <u>helped them much which had believed through grace:</u>

Notice that Apollos first preached the Gospel of the Kingdom, but Pricilla and Aquila took him aside. They taught him *the way of God more perfectly* for this

Age of Grace. As a result, Apollos became an excellent teacher and helped many to believe *through grace*.

There is a reason that Paul felt it was necessary to send additional teachers to the Corinthian assembly. 1 Corinthians 16:13-14:

> 13 **Watch ye, <u>stand fast in the faith</u>, quit you like men, be strong. 14 Let all your things be done with charity [love].**

Here is a story I would like to share with you. As I worked through the commentary, I apply the interpretation of Scripture by rightly dividing the Word of Truth. When I got to the above verse I felt that the Spirit wanted me to stop and so I did. These words prevented what, I believe, could have been a division in an assembly.

There was a misunderstanding among the believer in the church. People tend to choose who or which side they will support. I stopped to ponder the meaning of "quit like men." The word *quit* can mean *to stop or cease doing something* or it could mean *to leave or depart a place*. In view of the situation, for me, understanding its meaning was very powerful. It meant stop being "like men" with their pride and ego. Instead, everything is to be done with charity or love.

That is how any assembly should handle disagreements, differences, and expectations. When everyone focuses on Christ and His love, all differences seem to melt away. Next time there is a disagreement in your assembly, remember this. Stop being like men with pride, egos, and self-centeredness. Instead, remember this: *let all things be done with charity [love]*. I saw it work to the glory of God.

Paul gives an example of believers who became diligent workers in the ministry. Verses 15-16:

> 15 **I beseech you, brethren, (ye know the house of Stephanas, that it is the firstfruits of Achaia, and that they have addicted themselves to the ministry of the saints,)**
>
> 16 **That ye submit yourselves unto [doing] such, and to every one that helpeth with us, and laboureth.**

He implores them to be like others who work and labor for the furtherance of the Gospel of Grace. These three men to whom Paul refers had traveled to Corinth to assist with the building up of the faithful there. Verses 17-18:

> 17 **I am glad of the coming of Stephanas**

and Fortunatus and Achaicus: for that which was lacking on your part they have supplied. 18 For they have refreshed my spirit and yours: therefore acknowledge ye them that are such.

Paul is writing to them from Ephesus and sends greetings to the Corinthians from the fellow believers there in Asia Minor which is now Turkey. Verses 19-20:

19 The churches of Asia salute you. Aquila and Priscilla salute you much in the Lord, with the church that is in their house. 20 All the brethren greet you. Greet ye one another with an holy kiss.

The words *holy kiss* refer to a custom still used in many cultures today. The greeting requires two people to touch their opposite cheeks together as a *kiss* of peace. It is *holy* and, therefore, should be seen as physically pure and morally blameless.

With forged letters purporting to be from the Apostle Paul, he used his signature to authenticate his letters. Verse 21:

21 The salutation of me Paul with mine own hand.

Due to the solemn nature of his letter as to disobedient children, Paul writes what is a very stern warning. There are those who love the Lord and will follow Him and there are those who will choose not to love Him. To the latter, Paul writes in verse 22:

> 22 **If any man love not the Lord Jesus Christ, let him be Anathema Maranatha.**

The translators chose to leave two words in the original Greek: *anathema* and *maranatha*. The first means *let him be accursed*. The second means *the Lord cometh* or *the Lord will come*. We are told that the Lord will come and, when He does, He will judge those who rejected His love and gracious offer of salvation. As a result of their rejection, they will be *accursed*.

Paul follows this warning with a blessing upon all those who accept by faith the Gospel of Grace. Verse 23:

> 23 **The grace of our Lord Jesus Christ be with you. 24 My love be with you all in Christ Jesus. Amen.**

Epilogue

This letter to the Corinthians was written at the beginning of Paul's ministry. The city of Corinth was filled with pagan religions and practices. There were ample choices for those seeking the pleasures of the flesh. This is one of the first assemblies which accepted the preaching of the Gospel of Grace. They were a constant concern for Paul because of the challenges they faced. One theme that seems to flow throughout this letter is *the love of God*. This is the love which brought the Savior to give His life for sinners.

Paul seeks to help them deal with challenges of the world. Sinfulness was so prevalent in their society that they overlooked blatant sins of others within their assembly. This cannot be tolerated because it establishes an appearance of acceptance. Those who rebel against God must be put out of the assembly. This does not mean that the individual will lose their salvation if it was indeed genuine. However, they will be subject to the consequences of their actions.

Should they repent, they should be allowed to rejoin the assembly, All have sinned and fallen short of the glory, or perfection, of God.

Paul stresses the importance of correct doctrine. Those who change Paul's teachings are of the opposition and should not be allowed to teach in the assembly. In all things, love must prevail. This continues to be his message. We saw that the word *charity* is used by Paul to mean *love*. 1 Corinthians 13:13:

> **13 And now abideth faith, hope, charity, [love] these three; but the greatest of these is charity [love].**

One verse had an impact on my life. 1 Corinthians 16:13-14:

> **13 Watch ye, stand fast in the faith, quit you like men, be strong. 14 <u>Let all your things be done with charity [love].</u>**

I need to stand firm in the faith and know correct doctrine. Yet, I still think like a man with human emotions. I saw the word *quit* which means *to stop*. Therefore, when I encounter a problem, I need to stop thinking like a man, be strong in my faith, and not let anger or frustration overwhelm me.

I should do everything with love which is a central theme in this letter. Remember *the more excellent way?* It was about *love* –His *greatest gift.* God's love is unique. While we were still in our fallen state he loved us. Romans 5:8:

> **8 But God commendeth his love toward us, in that, while we were yet sinners, Christ died for us.**

God's love is constant and never changes! Paul is confident of this. Romans 8:38-39:

> **38 For I am persuaded, that neither death, nor life, nor angels, nor principalities, nor powers, nor things present, nor things to come,**

> **39 Nor height, nor depth, nor any other creature, shall be able to separate us from the love of God, which is in Christ Jesus our Lord.**

It was to the assembly having so much trouble with sin that Paul sent this letter of love. Who is better than Paul to show grace to others than the chief of sinners – a man who received love from the gracious Savior? I think it was fitting that Paul concluded his letter with this. 1 Corinthians 16:23-24:

23 The grace of our Lord Jesus Christ be with you. **24** My love be with you all in Christ Jesus. Amen

Maranatha!
Dr. David Alan Greene

Resources

Here are some resources I would recommend. My dear friends Steve and Stephanie Tackett offer many resources. Steve has taught rightly dividing the Word of Truth for many years. He breaks the Bible down and explains it dispensationally. He has written two of the books in the Grace Expositional Commentary Series. They offer live weekly online Bible classes, recorded classes, and audio recordings through Grace Bible Network. Their website is: www.gracebiblenetwork.org.

The Berean Bible Society has been helping people to understand right division since 1940. They mail out a free monthly publication called *The Berean Searchlight*. All you have to do is sign up for it online. They offer free online classes, have a bookstore, and host regional Bible conferences as well. Their website is: www.bereanbiblesociety.org.

There is a list of Grace Assemblies preaching the Word of God rightly divided. As of this writing, the list is maintained and updated regularly. Their website is: www.gracechurches.wordpress.com.

Finally, you can check out the list of other publications from GraceWord Publishing. Their website is: www.gracewordpublishing.com. There is a Contact Us option on the website.

Other GraceWord Publications

Cartas A Teofilo
Efesios: Dispensacionalmente considerado
El evangelio Oculto: Una vez fue un misterio . . .

About The Author

Dr. David Alan Greene has over thirty-five years of experience as an insurance agent selling both property and casualty as well as life insurance. During his career, he taught and explained the content and meaning of policies to his clients. Now retired, he devotes much of his time to teaching the Bible.

He obtained his Bachelor of Theology, Master of Biblical Studies, and Ph.D. in Biblical Studies from Evangelical Theological Seminary where he holds the position of Dean of Graduate Studies. He also holds a Ph.D. in Christian Counseling. He has written numerous biblical commentaries and books on rightly dividing the Word of Truth.

www.ingramcontent.com/pod-product-compliance
Lightning Source LLC
Chambersburg PA
CBHW060805120626
46557CB00001B/96